Kids and Computers

The Parents' Microcomputer Handbook

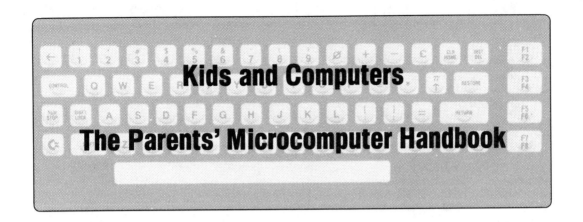

Kids and Computers

The Parents' Microcomputer Handbook

by Eugene Galanter, PhD

A GD/Perigee Book

Perigee Books
are published by
The Putnam Publishing Group
200 Madison Avenue
New York, New York 10016

IBM is a registered trademark of International Business Machines Corporation.
The name Apple and Apple Computer are registered trademarks of Apple Computer Inc.
CBM and PET are registered trademarks of Commodore Business Machines Corporation.
Cromemco is a trademark of Cromemco, Inc.
TRS-80 and Radio Shack are registered trademarks of Radio Shack, a division of Tandy Corporation.

Back cover photo by Gerald A. Tate
Cover photo courtesy of The Children's Computer School
Book design by Deb Loveless
Illustrations by Lowren West

Library of Congress Cataloging in Publication Data
Galanter, Eugene
     Kids and computers.

     Bibliography: p.
     Includes index.
     1. Computers and children. 2. Microcomputers.
I. Title
QA76.9.C659G34   1982   001.64   82-82310
ISBN 0-399-50749-3

First Perigee printing, 1983
Printed in the United States of America

1   2   3   4   5   6   7   8   9

To all my children.

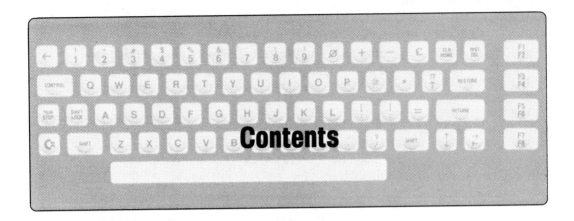

Contents

Preface

This book is for parents and youngsters. It will open the way for all of you to understand a technical explosion that could change the world. This book tells about microcomputers, those small keyboard-and-TV-screen machines that can play games, teach you the names of state capitals, drill you on multiplication tables, balance your checkbook, and help you and your children learn French. Not simply for microcomputer experts, the text is so organized that people who know little or nothing about microcomputers can enter into this sometimes frustrating and always fascinating enterprise.

I have designed this book to be a valuable resource for two broad categories of people: for parents and teachers who have little or no general knowledge of computers or programming and who want to acquire an understanding of what children are or should be learning from computer programs in the classroom, at camps, or at computer schools like The Children's Computer School. I recommend that you read Chapters 1, 2, 3, 8, 10, and 11, thoroughly and skim Chapters 4, 5, 6, 7, and 9. This will give you a good grasp of what microcomputers in children's education and recreation are all about, and I hope it will whet your appetite to sit down at a microcomputer keyboard and try it yourself.

The other category of readers this book addresses are those who have done just that! If you have had any practice with the machines, or are the proud owner of a personal home microcomputer, you will be especially interested in the hands-on programming information provided in Chapters 5, 6, 7, and 9. Of course, I hope the informative discussion in the remaining chapters will expand your interest and spur you to new heights in the creative use of microcomputers to teach and entertain kids.

In 1974 I ordered a minicomputer to control experiments in my research laboratory at Columbia University in New York. When it arrived, all silver and blue with a small calculatorlike keyboard on its face, we all gathered around to see it do its work. In went the plug, on went the switch . . . nothing happened. Out came the instruction manuals. Four hundred seventeen pages and seven weeks later we got the computer to work. Pressing key number 1 turned on a small light, the number 2 key turned it off. Our lab staff celebrated that afternoon. We had, amongst us, written a program in the machine's language to turn the light on and off. Four months after that, one of our group had written a program to do a serious piece of work. If this represented the return on investment for a minicomputer, we were in deep trouble.

Within a year the machine was running many experiments. I started to turn around in my opinions. It was still enormously difficult to write a bug-free program from scratch, but those we did write made all our work much easier. Just at that time I heard about a new machine that Radio Shack was planning to introduce. I obtained one of the first TRS-80s and found out about high-level programming languages like BASIC. What a revelation. I could write a clean program in two days. It became clear that these machines and others like them were destined for future glory.

When I realized that my general programming skill was attributable to the machine language I had been forced to use with the lab's first minicomputer, I looked over the Radio Shack machine, which came with an excellent instruction manual, and saw the truth. You had to learn to program even in BASIC. But if you first had to learn machine-language programming in order to learn BASIC programming it did not seem feasible for anyone—you, your kids, my kids—to be able to do it from a book. We needed a carefully designed, tested, and perfected curriculum aimed first at a high-level programming language that could teach us and our kids to program without the pain of confusion and failure. I went to work.

With my three daughters as my experimental subjects I designed and redesigned methods and techniques for teaching computer programming. Some of these techniques are so obvious that once they are displayed it is not clear why teaching computer programming seemed so difficult. But other aspects of programming skill are more subtle and recalcitrant to obvious formulations. The fact is that the learning

process for this skill changes the way you have to think.

We at The Children's Computer School are at work right now to develop and test the ramifications of some far-reaching educational consequences of the microcomputer invasion. One of the most unique contributions of the microcomputer in educational research is that when properly programmed the machine itself provides new and potentially profound measurement methods to assess the quantitative aspects of students' learning and thinking. Therefore the conjectures and other hypotheses put forward here will be testable with a precision not available before.

This book is the product of many collaborative efforts. Three of the collaborators—my daughters Michelle, Gabrielle, and Alicia—made their contributions indirectly. They served as the test cases for many of the principles that we now use to teach children computer programming. For these contributions I can only offer my thanks and love. My editor at Grosset and Dunlap, Adrienne Ingrum, gave her time and thought to the many revisions of the manuscript. The book itself is the consequence of all the thinking and discussion that my wife, Patricia, poured into it. She is the person who turns abstractions into reality. This book is concrete evidence of that fact.

Eugene Galanter

Introduction

Some Historical Notes

When Johann Gutenberg invented movable type for the printing press in 1438, he changed humankind. His invention brought about the third most fundamental technical revolution to have an impact on peoples' minds since the beginning of recorded history. The first, and undoubtedly most important, was the invention of writing itself. This monumental event, which I understand has only occurred a few times throughout history, is thought by some psychologists to have changed the intrinsic nature of the human mind. Recently, a British anthropologist has suggested (quite appropriately) that writing is the wedge that divides the primitive from the advanced, the barbarian from the civilized. Whatever its ramifications for the human spirit, there is no question of its technical importance in the advancement of human endeavor. Even my Columbia University colleague, Professor Henry Graff, who believes that literacy may have impeded individual social advancement in the nineteenth century, does not deny the correlation between literacy and social, political, and economic success.

The second technical revolution was the discovery of the applicability of mathematics to material things, such as measurement and navigation. From the calculations of the Nile River floods and the planning and construction of the pyramids, to the launch of the American Space Shuttle, mathematical calculations underlie all of humankind's major technical successes.

Although the first two revolutions were central to intellectual growth for the few, Gutenberg's invention reshaped society, as well as the human mind. When one's brain is exposed to the possible, many paths become actual. The power of knowledge diffusion that the printing press provides has contributed more to the human enterprise for more human beings than any other single technological force in history.

The widespread availability of knowledge and information that the printing press made possible led to incredible advances in understanding that precipitated revolutions, both bloody and peaceful. Literacy became the touchstone to democracy. The possibility of inexpensive books and the need for a literate labor force created the need for schools, and schools created new people—people who could learn throughout their lives. The contribution of the schools cannot be overestimated. We stand now at the threshold of a new age of literacy—computer literacy—whose demands on our schools, both now and in the immediate future, may well overshadow the demands of the past.

Kids and Computers

Children's needs for this new literacy are growing and will continue to grow. Our schools will be a central agent for this growth, and indeed the schools may find a new vitality in this new initiative. For this job, unlike some demands of the recent past, requires a marshaling of intellectual force.

My praise of printing is not intended to shortchange other socially important ideas. Indeed, the shape of our world depends not only on its technology, but on the purposes and applications of that technology. But without the techniques, ideas have a rough row to hoe. So we begin this venture into a new field by acknowledging immediately the debt of the present to the workers of the past. The dissemination of information has in the past been recognized as central to the growth, development, control, and extension of the human hand on the face of the earth. The fourth revolution, our current leap ahead into the age of the computer, will, in my view, take its place with the other three as the shaper of a new society.

The modern digital computer developed from ideas contained in such mundane practical devices as the Jacquard weaving looms of the 1790s. Patterns to be woven into cloth were coded by holes punched into cards. These cards served as a *program* to control the shuttles that carried differently colored warps across the loom. The actual conception of a modern computer controlled by such punched cards was proposed by an Englishman, Charles Babbage, in 1821. He died in 1871, after failing to complete a successful "analytical engine." The record of his work was preserved for us by Augusta Ada, Lady Lovelace, who was the only child of Lord and Lady Byron.

The idea of punching holes in cards to store information was taken up and used in the United States by Herman Hollerith. Hollerith, a graduate of Columbia University, developed a tabulating machine to help in the analysis of United States census data. Such punched-card tabulating systems were continuously improved to form the basis of useful business machines. When Hollerith's Tabulating Machine Company, joined forces with a time-clock manufacturer to form International Business Machines Corporation, the connection between American business enterprise and computing machinery was firmly established. The new president of IBM, Thomas Watson, Sr., was an early sponsor of academic research into computers and computing machinery. He gave several million dollars in grants to Howard Aiken at Harvard University. Those gifts underwrote the development of an early computing machine—the Harvard Mark I.

Some of the main principles of computer design were already in place when Alan Turing wrote a seminal article on the theory of computers in 1937. But it wasn't until 1945, when J. Presper Eckert and John W. Mauchly at the Moore School of Engineering at the University of Pennsylvania completed their work for the United States Army on a functional multipurpose digital computer—ENIAC— Electronic Numerical Integrator And Calculator, that the age of computers can be said to have arrived.

Those first computers filled huge caverns with their bulk. The air-conditioning systems they needed to keep cool were as powerful as those needed for a twenty-story office building. But the transistor, developed by William Shockley at the Bell Telephone Laboratories in 1948, started a miniaturizing and energy-saving movement that has not yet reached a limit. The transistor is a device to modulate or control the flow of an electric current.

Like the vacuum tube it replaced, it makes possible the amplification and switching of electrical signals. Whereas the transistor was a replacement for the vacuum tube, the integrated circuit replaced a whole network of thousands of transistors and other electrical components with a single chip of silicon. It is the integrated circuit that shrank those massive mastodons to packing-crate size—still not your friendly portable typewriter, but not bad. By 1970, computer hobbyists had devised useful, if limited, computers that would fit on a tabletop. These models served as prototypes for today's Apples, PET®s, and TRS-80s.

Figure 1: The ENIAC at the Moore School of Electrical Engineering, University of Pennsylvania. It was one of the first successful digital computers in the world.

Kids and Computers

The existence of a computer you can carry changed the notion of who uses a computer. Originally it was a special task reserved for the high priests of the computer center. Now the codes needed to program the computer to work had to be adapted for popular consumption. This had been taken care of in 1967 by John Kemeny, who before becoming Dartmouth College's president had devised a programming *language* called BASIC. The word BASIC is an acronym for Beginners All-purpose Symbolic Instruction Code. As we shall see presently, it is at once the simplest, but often the most irritating, programming language around. Although there is always talk of changing or replacing it as the benchmark of programming languages, BASIC is now so widely used and popular that it is truly the standard. One feature of BASIC that we find helpful at The Children's Computer School is that the command vocabulary is English. This means that our kids not only learn to program easily, they also learn a collection of (often new) words and phrases.

The computer is making its way into every home and work place. As a consequence, computer literacy becomes a necessary skill. Just as printing made the written word available to all and the ability to read and write a necessity and not a privilege, so also has the desk-top computer made computing skills essential. But it is more than just a skill to help us get along with a new machine, for after all, typewriters give us that opportunity. Rather, understanding computers and how they do our work opens new possibilities to enhance our understanding and comprehension of things in general.

These comments might also be appropriate to describe all of this electronic age. Movies, TV, radio, stereo, and other media for entertainment and enlightenment have had profound effects on our lives. But my point is that these media require only the most minimal skills above simple perception to be appreciated. It is the lack of demand that they may make on our intellectual capacities that leads critics to call them "passive informers." Children especially watch and listen only for the "line," and not for the meaning. This results in commercial productions that are attractive but only minimally demanding. On the other hand, computers, even computer games, require more than mere perception of the surrounding scene. Some intellectual effort and motor coordination are necessary to enjoy using these devices. The conclusion seems reasonable: Among the products of the new electronic age, the home computer can contribute more to a child's intellectual development than can existing media programming.

The microcomputer is not merely a new device; it is the realization of a new mode of thinking and acting. Let your child neglect this skill and he or she becomes as handicapped as an illiterate. Now these are strong statements. In what follows I shall demonstrate beyond any doubts you may now have that, if anything, the case is understated. So the stage is set for what I hope will be a lively and interesting introduction for you and your child to the new world of computing and computers. Let us turn now to what computer literacy is, what it does for a child's ability to think and act, and how it can shape our ways of thinking about all sorts of things, computable or not.

Chapter 1

Microcomputers and Your Child

As the director of a school that teaches computer programming to children I am often asked, "What use is it for my child to learn to program a computer?" That question often launches a long discussion, because there are many answers. To some parents I need only say, "It will open up job opportunities." If pressed for details, I remark on the need for programmers, *software* (program) writers, computer sales and service personnel, and other contributors to the microcomputer revolution. For other parents the value resides in the obvious pleasure the child gets from messing around with a computer. Most kids just love to work at a computer, either playing games, just making it work, or watching it spin out some results from a program. These kids want to learn to program computers for the sheer fun of it.

But if the conversation flows, we get down to the features of programming skill that may have more important consequences for the child's mental development, because writing successful computer programs means:

1. Your child will learn to operate a keyboard skillfully.

2. Your child will discover that spelling mistakes (and other kinds of errors) will not be tolerated.

3. Your child will grasp the logical flow of complicated thoughts.

4. Your child will be forced to unravel broad general problems into small steps.

5. Your child will find that rewards for partial success and powerful rewards for final victory are sweet.

6. Your child will learn that his or her programming work can be embellished and polished to enhance its performance.

7. Your child will develop various aesthetic skills and judgment.

(And remember that you, the parent, will reap similar rewards if you join your child in his or her programming endeavors.)

These skills and abilities are valuable for their importance to a variety of life's problems. Indeed, such skills lie at the base of many intellectual and technical tasks. The unraveling of complicated questions into sequences of simple ones is the mark of intellectual power in many realms of endeavor. This cognitive ability is a necessity for writers of computer programs, and from our experience it seems to grow with practice in programming. Not only does the writing of programs enhance the writer's cognitive ability in the abstract, but because many programs that children write are designed to help them with substantive school problems, there is a free ride on substance. For example, my eldest daughter, Alicia, worked for five afternoons on a program to test for and teach knowledge of Latin declensions. By the time the program was running successfully, she no longer needed it. Friends in her class used the program for its intended purposes. I cannot say whether they spent more or less time than Alicia did, but she had the fun of two successes for the price of one.

Computers at home can shore up educational deficiencies by providing what has been named *computer-aided instruction,* or *CAI.* The fact of the matter is that CAI is nothing more nor less than a way to study. In CAI the materials to be mastered have been arranged in a logical order and require keyboard inputs from the student so that testing and teaching go on at the same time. Materials for such instruction come packaged for many home computers in the form of educational programs. These computer programs are often ingenious and playfully integrated with graphic displays to enhance the motivations of the child. Some are primarily technical, and are used, for example, to prep for such achievement and aptitude tests as the Scholastic Aptitude Test and the Graduate Record Examination. Parents tell me that when they help their children with such programs they often learn new concepts. Best of all, from my experience, is for you and your children to write programs for CAI together. In homes where older and younger children are together, the older and wiser ones often write programs to help their younger siblings with their schoolwork. One reason that I strongly favor writing your own CAI is because the quality of the available materials is quite low. It is hard to maintain a child's interest with many currently available instructional programs. On the other hand, a program you write yourself to teach and test for multiplication skills is valuable, not only as a teacher, but as an object of your own creation.

The emotional rewards of a successful program are large. Even the ability to make part of a program operate, or *run* as we call it, calls for a minor internal celebration. This taste of success compensates for the very large effort that writing these programs requires. But there is more than the feeling of success; there is the consequence of effort. Often, in traditional school subjects, the effort expended generates very little obvious return. But a running program is something to see! I have observed a young person write a video-game program, which to me seemed to be a bore. But when it ran, the look of ecstasy on the programmer's face made more light than the video tube. Not every child responds this way to the programming experience, but even those who do not, find an advantage in the work.

Programming a microcomputer requires the entry of letters and numbers by pressing keys that are arranged much like a typewriter keyboard. One fact about the programming effort is that time seems to go too fast. You want to see whether your program is working, but you cannot until you finish the typing. The result for a child is that great skill in keyboard entry is acquired at an early age—not touch typing you understand, but key locations and speed of entry. I am not sure whether this aids or impairs subsequent learning of touch typing, but my guess is that it may not matter. The winds of change in keyboard design are in the air. Skill may be necessary to key in data in new kinds of formats, but there may be less demand for the ability to enter text at high speed. Do not misunderstand these remarks. There is no question that touch-typing skill is now and will continue to be a useful ability. My remarks are directed only to suggest that even if early keyboard use makes it harder to learn to type, it repays the trade-off by improving general keyboard skill.

A final point concerns a subtle skill that grows as a child gains experience. This ability involves the aesthetics of programming. A computer, and especially a microcomputer, is limited by various factors. These include the size of its memory, the number and kind of commands it can execute, the number of operations and functions it can perform, and so on. Luckily, a program to do a certain piece of work can be written in a variety of ways, just as a poem or a musical sonata can. This means that you will have to work out procedures to accomplish your goals within the limits of your computer. Some ways of getting there are clumsy and inefficient; other paths are elegant. One quickly learns to recognize the difference between the clear-cut wheat and the obvious chaff, but doing the right stuff is the mark of skill. The ability to function effectively within a set of accepted limitations is the mark of the artist. This ability is as important in computing as it is in music or painting. The study of computer programming develops this skill and offers this reward.

The previous comments suggest the importance of programming as an aid to cognitive development, emotional adventure, motor control, and fine motor skills. You should also notice that these skills serve to take the mystery out of computers and also out of certain aspects of quantitative knowledge.

Let us start with computers. Once a person has written a program even at the simplest level, the use of any computer becomes a manageable concept. What the computer does is clear to the child. This means that poorly informed remarks about computers and their implications for society can be evaluated intelligently by the child programmer. For example, no one can convince our students that the *computer* made a "mistake" by spelling their names wrong on a mailing list. I can hear my daughter Michelle now: "Bad input prompts."

The solutions to complicated mathematical problems were an early impetus to the development of computers. Even today, many people believe that there is a strong connection between computers and mathematics. On the one hand this is true, in the same sense that landing astronauts on the moon is a mathematical problem. But an astronaut may or may not be a mathematician. Just because the systems he uses are guided by material expressions of mathematical equations does not mean that he literally flies on a formula. The same is true of computers. They rest on profound mathematical ideas, but like a rocket ship (or an automobile), you can drive one without solving the equations.

Take an example we use in our school. We ask our students to write a program that will calculate how much money they will have in their savings account if they deposit a certain amount each month and receive interest income each year. Now we all know there is a formula to solve that problem complete with parentheses and exponents and such. But to the computer, which couldn't care less about formulas, the program can be written using only multiplication (for the interest) and addition (to increase the balance). The reason is that the computer can "simulate" the time that passes, replacing each year with a sixtieth of a second. In this way the problem is solved directly. Multiply the interest rate by the current balance, and add that amount to the old balance to make a new current balance. Do that as many times as you need to, and lo! the answer pops up in less than a second.

All this talk about computers and the value of learning to program them represents the intellectual side of this whole enterprise. But there is another side that concerns sharing. The parents of a child who is learning to program a computer can enter into this world more easily than they can enter into most of a child's activities. The reason for this is simple. Computers easily become a focus of activity for many aspects of family life. And unlike the TV, the computer is an interactive device. It requires input while it provides output. This aspect of computers and computing is what gives this activity its unique quality. The father of one of our students took a course at our school to learn all about word processing. As a result, he bought a small computer to use at home for his technical writing. His 14-year-old son used the machine for games and programming exercises. As the father tells the story, one evening he remarked at dinner that he wished the computer could handle the family accounts, but all he could do with it was write articles. His son said he could write the program. The family sat down around the machine together, and over the next few months they hammered out a simple but effective program to maintain the family finances, including the household checkbook and their tax records.

Consider the advantages that this family received from their home computer. They shared an activity together that was of importance to the family as a whole. The

son had a valuable programming experience—he devised a way to process family accounts. In the course of this programming experience, he also learned something about family finances and felt a part of the enterprise that the family budget represents.

So not only can games and puzzles be played on the machine, but record keeping (including such things as Christmas card lists, menus and recipes, and the Little League standings) and schoolwork are also usefully augmented by computer programs. As in the previous story, many aspects of family life can be refined and made simple and pleasurable by developing and using a computer program. And although programs to do these various chores can be purchased, many of them are so simple and straightforward to write that the programming task can become a family adventure. I have a friend who makes finely detailed scale models for people who have boats. John remarked that he never had a mailing-label program that worked the way he wanted it to until he took our intermediate programming course. John himself finally wrote the program he really wanted.

Such fancy programs as video games may be beyond a youngster's current programming skills, but thousands of programs (many written by kids like yours) can be purchased to operate on a home machine. These store-bought programs can make your computer into a household appliance that will compete favorably in usefulness with the dishwasher or the vacuum cleaner. Other components that connect to these microcomputers enable your machine to communicate over your telephone line with big *mainframe* computers that can provide programs for your own machine, as well as information ranging from current stock prices to the news of the day. One such service,

CompuServe Inc. of Columbus, Ohio, offers a national "CB" system that lets computer hobbyists from all over the United States "talk" to each other for the price of a local phone call and a modest hourly connect charge.

You may well ask then, "If all these programs are available and simply plug in or whatever to a computer, why do I or my child need to learn to program?" One kind of answer is that even the best current programs for doing things you want and need to do may have to be adapted to your specific requirements. And this state of the art is likely to continue into the future. Most important, however, is the fact that knowing how to program reveals the nature of the machine in a way that commercially available programs do not. Finally, it comes down to this: Literacy has always meant that you know how to write as well as read. You may not write your own novels, but you do write your own notes. To my mind the same principle holds for computer literacy. You may not write commercial programs, but being able to write programs lets you take charge.

The important point to remember about your child as a programmer is that the skill develops slowly. It is most important that parents encourage their children, even when the results are (to us) quite simpleminded. As we have seen, a small taste of success breeds larger projects. A simple three-line program that merely prints out the child's name over and over again may serve to motivate further progress. Not every session at the computer ends in success. Often a problem bounces around a child's head for several days, or even weeks. Finally, an insight or something like it occurs, and then the program comes pouring out. We do not know what leads to these spurts, but they are common and easily recognized. A bit of parental

encouragement and praise is never out of place.

The other side of the coin is to avoid pressing a child to overwork at the machine. The last thing any child needs is to believe that your approval depends on the quality or quantity of his or her work. A question about progress is never out of place, but constant surveillance and pressure to perform have as bad an effect on computer programming as they do on music lessons or sports. The challenge and the pressure must come from within.

Perhaps at this point it will be helpful to list by a child's age what can be expected in the way of computer literacy. We shall assume for the purpose of our exposition that the child is instructed in computer use by a qualified teacher using a sound curriculum. At The Children's Computer School, 5-year-olds learn to load programs into a machine and to operate it to play instructional games. Some of these instructional programs in math and reading readiness were written by our older students. The 5-year-olds also learn the location of keys on the keyboard, as well as how to read simple instructions on the computer screen. By the age of 8, our students are ready to learn to write their own simple programs. At about 11, many of our kids are prepared to develop complex programs and may even begin to design computer program "suites," to perform very complex tasks, such as graphics games, data-base management systems, and so on. At 14 they begin to pass their instructors.

I recall a meeting of a local computer club in New York, at which the average age of the membership was about 40. Most of the people there had only recently purchased their machines, but they were caught up in the spirit of discovery and had formed the club to learn more about

Table 1
Children's Programming Skills

AGE		COMPUTER SKILL	OPERATE	PROGRAMMING
years	months	(input-output)	SOFTWARE	(commands)
5	0	Keyboard letter locations	No	None
5	6	Letter & number keypad	Some	None
6	0	Keying spelling words	Yes	LOAD
6	4	Reading and keying	Yes	LOAD-STOP
6	8	Read, Key, and Respond	Yes	3 commands
7	6	Manage programs	Yes	SAVE
8		10- to 20-line programs	Data Base	7 commands
9		Sorts and searches	Word Proc	Lists, tables
10-12		50- to 100-line programs	Any	File manage
13 plus		Files and data base	M. L.	Machine language

Note: This table represents averages of abilities reported by teachers at The Children's Computer School.

how their machines worked. The lecture that evening was given by a 14-year-old. This is a young technology, easily mastered by the young. Often the young are the ones who know most about new techniques and methods. I had installed a new machine in our laboratory at Columbia University during the summer of 1978 but could not find any of our graduate students or under-graduates who knew the ins and outs of the new machine. After confessing my desperate need to my wife Patricia, she found a consultant who knew my machine inside and out, a local high school student.

Before I leave this topic let us address the question of sex. As you know, there is an old wives' tale that girls are not as adept at mathematics as boys. I am not prepared to either affirm or deny this view, but I can speak with certainty about girls and computers. Our current split in the enrollment at The Children's Computer School is about 40% girls. Their performance is, if anything, better than the boys'. I think the enrollment figures reflect that some girls may be concerned about their ability in this area. I enter these remarks here for you to convey to your daughters if they express such concerns. One of my colleagues who asserts that girls are indeed less able in math also states with equal vigor that he is sure they are better at computer programming. On the last part of his assertions I agree wholeheartedly.

By this time I hope you have a taste of the issues we shall confront as we move through this new world of microcomputers. The personal computer era has dawned. This era brings with it new devices with properties and qualities never before seen in a mechanical device. These qualities and properties will form the basis of our exploration into this new world of computer literacy. It is probably not too great an exaggeration to say that this new tool and its use by us, the common man, will reconstruct the nature of our relations to each other and to the world at large. It is still too early to see the final shape of this new structure, but here and there the shadows of the future are discernible. We shall explore both the present as it is and the future as it may become. We may not see this voyage of imagination proceed, but for sure our children will.

What I have called the new computer literacy is not a product of the computer as such; the Sperry, IBM, and Control Data behemoths have been around for almost thirty-five years. The need for computer literacy is a product of the *micro*computer, what someone has called "a computer small enough to hug." The microcomputer is of fairly recent origin. We can date it from the first appearance of the Commodore PET®, the Radio Shack TRS-80, and the Apple—say 1976, give or take a year. These machines in turn came from the interests of small groups of computer hobbyists who provided a market for computer *chips.* Tiny integrated electronic circuit components encased in a plastic "centipede" were originally fashioned for military and space applications. These *integrated circuits* were a technological enhancement of the original *transistor.* The transistor you may recall was the solid-state miniaturized replacement of the vacuum tube, the original radio tube that paved the way for radio, television, and computers.

The central point to understand about these circuits is that they are *digital,* and not *analog.* Now what on earth does that mean? We know about digital watches, but what exactly is digital? First let us clear up analog. That term means

"varies in a continuous way." It is commonly associated with the measures of things, so weight, for example, is an analog quantity. So is height. So is the course of the movement of the planets. Indeed almost everything in the world of nature is analog. Plants grow in an analog way, as do children.

Digital on the other hand, means roughly, "varies discretely." A digital system has several clearly distinguishable states of being. That digital watch of yours does not show the exact time, because no matter how finely it displays the time, it shows only, say 9:06:37, a discrete time. These microchips are the same, except that their possible states of being are very few—two to be exact. The switches inside these chips can be either *on* or *off.* They are *Binary Digital* devices.

In order to understand the importance of these digital electronic chips and their relation to microcomputers, you must first become acquainted with the main features of a computer—any computer.

Every computer has four main parts:

1. a keyboard to get information into the computer
2. a video screen or a printer to get processed information out of the computer

Figure 2: The large-scale integrated circuit shown here contains a complete computer. Intel Corporation's MCS-48 single chip microcomputer. (Photo courtesy of Intel Corporation)

3. a central processing unit to work on the incoming information and make or recall the outgoing information
4. a storage system or memory to store the instructions for processing the information, and to store the information itself

Figure 3 shows these four parts and how they connect together.

Let us examine first the *central processing unit* and the memory, and skip the input (keyboard) and the output (printer or screen) for the moment because these are similar to things we already know about.

The input, after all is said and done, is very much like a typewriter; the output is like a small TV. The central processing unit, or CPU, is the computer. It is fabricated on a chip of silicon that is etched photographically with circuits of great complexity. The CPU chip represents many tens or even hundreds of thousands of transistors and constitutes a member of the LSI (large-scale integrated) family of devices. The chip itself contains several memories and also circuits that can address other memory located outside the CPU in other parts of the computer.

The CPU performs a variety of tasks. Some of these jobs, such as comparing two numbers to see if they are the same, are handled by the CPU itself. Others, such as getting a number stored in the main computer memory and copying it into its own memory, depend on the fact that the CPU can communicate with the main computer memory. Indeed, the special quality of the CPU is that it can copy the contents of any memory cell in the computer into itself, and conversely can send a copy of anything it contains to any memory cell in the computer. I always imagine the CPU as the main office of the computer. If I press a key on the computer's keyboard, the CPU reads the key from a small memory called the *keyboard buffer.* If the key (which has been coded by the keyboard buffer into a number) represents a letter or number that should appear on the computer's video screen, the CPU sends a command to the video screen memory to display the reencoded number as a *real letter* on the screen. The CPU does all the executive work in the computer, as well as making all the numerical calculations that the computer performs.

The main computer memory may be thought of as shelf after shelf after shelf of empty boxes. I think of them as shoe

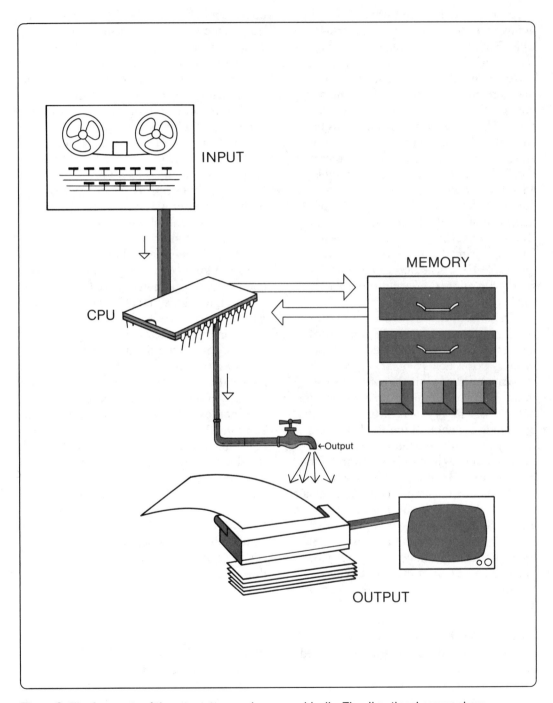

INPUT

MEMORY

CPU

Figure 3: The four parts of the computer are shown graphically. The directional arrows show the direction of information flow.

boxes, because they are rather small; also in my mind they are long rather than wide. Each box has a name on it (a number, really) that represents its address. In the current generation of microcomputers there are at most 65,536 of these memory boxes. This is because the current generation of CPUs can only remember this many addresses. This number may seem large, and indeed it is. For many jobs a computer is called on to do, this much memory is a kind of overkill. Yet even this current limit on memory size is bypassed in the next generation of microcomputers like the IBM Personal Computer which uses a CPU that can address more memory; or the Apple III, or the SuperPET® 9000 which can address a larger memory in smaller blocks.

The size of the memory in a microcomputer is measured by the number of memory boxes it contains. Each of these memory boxes holds 8 binary digits, or *bits,* as computerists and mathematicians call them. This word comes from a contraction of the words *BInary digiTS.* It was invented by Claude Shannon of the Bell Telephone Laboratories, who coined it to represent the fundamental unit of information. One bit, yes or no, on or off, up or down: It divides the world and our ignorance in half.

An 8-bit memory box is itself called a *byte.* So the current generation of microcomputers contain at most 65,536 bytes of memory. Since most microcomputers have at least a thousand bytes of memory, the unit of memory size is usually 1000. In metric lingo the *Kilo* prefix represents 1000, so the computer fraternity uses the letter *K* to mean "one thousand." Notice also that the numbers are rounded down from their exact values, so that 65,536 becomes 64K of memory.

The CPU can change the name on the box (or a whole row of them) from its address location number(s) to an arbitrary name that you, the user, can assign. This means that you can find the box(es) you want by this name rather than its address. You do not have to work through all the addresses to fetch or store a particular piece of information. However, you can also address the memory locations directly with special codes, called *PEEK*s, to get, and *POKE*s, to put, information into specific memory locations.

Because you can get information out of this computer memory, or *read* it, and also put information into it, or *write* to it, this class of memory can be thought of as *read-write memory.* There is usually a second kind of memory in many microcomputers whose memory contents cannot be changed. This memory is called *read-only memory* or ROM. We shall talk about ROM in greater detail later.

The read-write memory stores and accesses its information at random. This means that the CPU uses memory as it is needed, and just because two things go together logically does not mean they will be remembered at nearby addresses. The computer stores information without regard to relevance. Because of this unpatterned, or random, memory assignment it is not much of a surprise to find that this memory is called *random access memory,* or RAM. We can summarize this heavy bout with memory by remembering that in general the memory of a computer is of three kinds:

1. a small working memory in the CPU that is used for computation and information processing

2. RAM—random access memory— used to store and retrieve information and program instructions. It is a read-write memory.

3. ROM—read-only memory—used to store permanent instructions for the computer's general housekeeping operations

You should note that each memory box is so small that it can only hold a single letter. Recall that it is only 8 bits long. Indeed several memory boxes are needed to store any number, even a small one. To store your name would take as many memory boxes as there are letters in your name. The addresses of the memory boxes are rewritten as a simple name, rather than as a specific address; thus the CPU when told to "print your name" finds the right memory in the right order right away.

All this talk about what the CPU can do with the memory boxes sounds as though this machine may have a mind of its own. Some people believe this, but then some people believe in ghosts. A computer (from biggest to smallest) is simply a machine. It is a machine in the same sense as a vacuum cleaner or a refrigerator. The property that it possesses that puts it in a special category is that what it does can be changed. On Monday it may balance your checkbook; on Tuesday it may print out mailing labels; on Wednesday it may sort your recipe collection by country of origin or by meal course; on Thursday it may help the children with their homework; on Friday it can serve as an electric correcting typewriter; and on Saturday, or perhaps Sunday, it can serve as the family game center. But as has been briefly mentioned, all this frenzied activity depends on one aspect of the computer—it can store in its RAM the instructions (usually one set at a time) that are necessary to perform all these (and infinitely more) tasks. These stored and replaceable instructions are called programs.

They are what make computers unique. The refrigerator has a stored program. Its program instructs the machine to turn on the compressor when the temperature inside gets too high and to turn it off when the inside temperature is low enough. But you cannot reprogram the refrigerator to wash the dishes—too bad. It does not have replaceable programs.

One way to get off on the wrong foot with computers is to believe that they are mathematical machines or that you have to be a mathematician to use them. As remarked in the first chapter, nothing could be further from the truth. There is no question that when computers first came into prominence they were used mostly by mathematicians to solve mathematical problems. That is because they are good at it. But computers are not merely calculators; they are information processors. The information they process may be numerical, in which case they calculate, but the information can also be words and things like words, and when they process words they manipulate symbols. For example, suppose you have a computer that is programmed to maintain a list of data about your friends. You may type in their names, addresses, and telephone numbers in any order you choose along with birthdays, anniversaries, and special diet restrictions. You may then wish to get them out in some special order, e.g., first everybody in the 212 telephone area code, then the people in the 516 area, then the 914, and finally all the rest. Or perhaps you want to send birthday cards. You need your list sorted by birthdate. Any computer can do all this neatly and cleanly. Notice that there is no math visible in any of this.

One of the children in our school had a spelling problem with his regular school word lists. He often reversed letters or dropped a needed vowel. One of my teachers noticed that he rarely misspelled the program code words. We thought perhaps it was because he had to type them into the computer and check them before pressing a special key. With the child himself helping, the teacher wrote a program that required the computer to store the spelling lists. It would then flash a random word to the video screen for a fraction of a second. The child had to type in the word from the keyboard, and the computer checked the spelling against the word list. I would like to report that the child won a spelling bee; not quite, but he did meet his regular school requirements in spelling. The point of this story is not merely that computers can teach spelling, but that no math or computation was involved in the program.

Sometimes programs are a combination of calculation and information processing. If you use your computer to manage your household accounts, balancing your checkbook, and maintaining a file of deductible and nondeductible expenditures, the program requires the computer to add and subtract, as well as to label the expenses. But also notice that a well-programmed computer actually isolates you from the arithmetic of these procedures. You merely enter the amounts of deposits and checks; the computer performs the arithmetic and files the information behind the scenes, so to speak.

We have seen that the microcomputer can calculate, but it can also do much more. To appreciate some of these qualities, we must return to a consideration of the input and output systems of a computer, and then add some extra features that most computers need and use. We get information into a computer in two quite different ways; first and most obviously, through whatever keyboardlike device it may have as its input system. Usually this device is similar to a typewriter keyboard, even to the arrangement of the alphabet keys with the second row starting Q W E R T Y. Now you know why they call this a *qwerty keyboard.* Often there are extra keys of one kind or another. Commonly the number keys are duplicated and grouped together on the right side like an adding machine keyboard. This *numeric keypad* is used when the entry of lots of numbers is needed as in statistics or banking. Other keys are for special computer commands such as [CONTROL], which is a kind of special shift key that changes the meaning of other keys.

As an input system this typewriter is hard to beat. But recall our name and address list. What happens to the names and addresses (and telephone numbers and birthdays) as they are typed into the machine? As you might guess they are stored in those memory boxes. But observe that if each friend requires, say 35 memory cells for his name, another 35 more for the address, 25 for city, state, and zip code, another 15 for the birthday, and 12 for a telephone number, we will use more than 120 boxes per entry. The program of instructions itself resides in this memory and may occupy perhaps 10K bytes of memory. The ROM memory uses perhaps 20K for its own purposes. That leaves room for about 250 names—a lot, but not an awful lot. Even if this number is sufficient today, what do we do when we want a new program to run tomorrow?

Obviously a useful program and its input *data,* which are what we call the names and addresses, cannot remain in our computer permanently or it will never be able to do anything else. For this reason all computers since the earliest ENIAC that Eckert and Mauchley built in the late 1940s, have made use of special memory storage systems that are separate from

Figure 4: A computer keyboard that shows the qwerty layout. The 16 keys on the right side are a number key-pad that duplicate the number keys along the top row, but make the entry of numbers easier. (Photo courtesy of Franklin Computer Corporation)

the main computer memory. In the ENIAC these separate memory systems were usually magnetic devices. In those days they were rotating magnetic drums. Even today, magnetic storage is the most common separate memory system. Such systems store much more information than the RAM of the computer to which they are attached. For this reason they are dubbed *peripheral mass storage systems.* Whereas today the big machines use large tape recorders, today's microcomputers use cassette tape recorders as the least expensive way to perform this function. Other devices that we will talk about later, such as floppy disks and Winchesters, are also used as mass storage systems for microcomputers.

Once we introduce a mass storage memory to store the contents of the computer's RAM *off-line,* that is, out of the computer, we can also use it to store much more data than the computer can handle at one time. These additional data can be loaded into the computer as needed by the work the program in the computer is doing. To summarize this important point: Computers must remember the instructions they are to perform—their program; the computer must also remember the data these instructions work on. Both the data and the program can be stored outside the computer itself on a mass storage device. These devices are commonly magnetic tape or disk systems. Usually the storage system distinguishes between data and programs, although the computer itself does not. To the computer data can be used to instruct the machine, and segments of the instructions can be used as data. This subtle point is important to the computer, but not to you. The important point for you to remember is that data and programs are fundamentally different beasts.

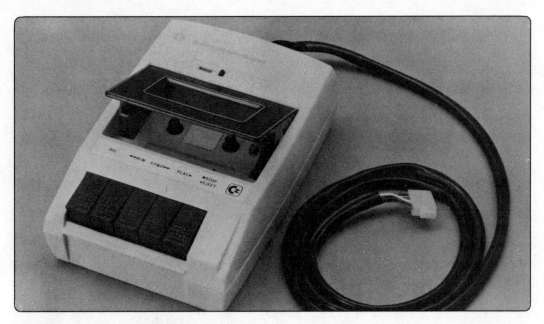

Figure 5: A cassette deck designed as a mass-storage system for a microcomputer. (Photo courtesy of Commodore Business Machines Inc.)

The existence of mass storage systems means that the internal working memory of the computer (sometimes called *core* or *core memory*)—the RAM—does not have to be as large as one might think. Generally speaking, a microcomputer with 8K of addressable RAM is quite adequate for someone starting out in programming. With clever programming that makes intelligent use of off-line storage in the mass storage system, 32K of RAM provides enough internal storage for almost any chore a microcomputer is likely to perform. For example, the word processor I used to write this book had 32K of available RAM. A limit of 32K of RAM permits the computer manufacturer to use up to 32K of memory for ROM storage in the current generation of machines. Sometimes manufacturers do not install any dedicated memory in ROM, in which case if all memory is RAM, the operator

must get the system started by loading a special program into RAM before he or she starts to use the machine. This is called *booting* the operating system. A popular microcomputer, the highly portable Osborne 1 uses such a procedure.

The peripheral mass storage system is the second way that information can be put into a machine. The first was through the keyboard. For example, the computer program to maintain our address list may be stored on mass storage and loaded into the computer first. The program itself will then direct the computer to load the data for use by the program from the same mass storage system. After the data have been processed by the program, for example, rearranged into alphabetical order, the program may then direct the computer to re-store the data back into mass storage. Notice that the rearranged data are stored as a new file onto the mass storage device. Now the storage system has twice the amount of information that was entered from the keyboard. This really is new information. The computer did not multiply the information like carbon paper or a copying machine. The computer actually worked on the information to turn it into a different form or format.

Most microcomputers use a television-like video screen as the primary output from the CPU. This is certainly a convenient and inexpensive way to see the letters and the numbers that the computer generates. In the not-so-distant past most computers used printing devices much like a typewriter for computer output. These *printer terminals* had the advantage of providing *hard copy* of the computed information, which is often a desirable end product. But they can generate enormous amounts of paper with very little information per page. After all, much of a computer's activity is highly transient. Who needs a printout of Dungeons and Dragons? And there is not much use in a printed copy of each deposit amount and check amount in your checkbook program. On the other hand, just seeing the video image of a report of your monthly deposits and withdrawals may not be enough to permit a careful reconciliation of your accounts with the bank statement. The same principle holds for educational programs. There is obviously little need to print every arithmetic problem your child has tried. On the other hand, it may be useful to print a cumulative score in order to chart progress.

Figure 6: This printer has sprockets to advance the specially punched paper. The holes along the edges of the paper can be torn off. (Photo courtesy of Cromemco Inc.)

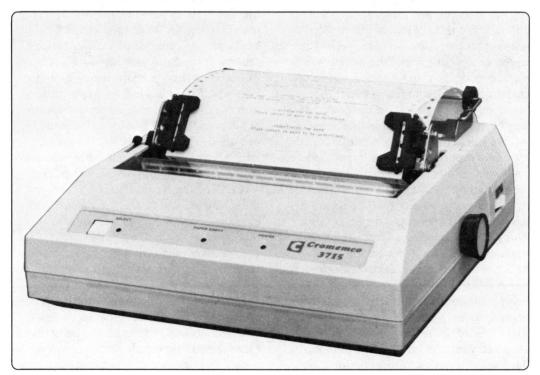

Consequently, the second most popular peripheral device for a microcomputer is a peripheral printer to provide hard copy of output when needed. Obviously, if the computer is going to be used primarily for video games, or more seriously for homework practice and skill drill, a printer may be unnecessary. But if permanent records of computed output are needed, then a printer is mandatory.

Once you or your children get involved in programming, there is a use for a simple printer that is unrelated to printing out data and reports. A printer is a valuable asset for printing out the program code or listing of your program. As we shall see when we turn to programming itself, the program in the computer can be *listed,* by the simple command, LIST, usually to the video screen for editing or other needed changes. However, trying to keep track of all the program when you can only see one screenful at a time is difficult. For this reason an inexpensive printer that can copy the contents of the screen or the contents of the computer's memory is often a useful tool. Such printers may not print on regular paper, but rather on treated paperlike material that may be electrically etched by the print mechanism. The real cost of these devices is usually supplying them with their special paper, which is more expensive than paper used by impact inked-ribbon printers.

A new peripheral input-output device has been gaining in popularity recently. This is the speech synthesizer. As a specialized output system it can be seen in daily use as part of the Texas Instruments' Speak & Spell teaching toy. Insofar as many educational applications of microcomputers may depend on hearing the spoken word, these new synthesizers to attach to your computer may be among the most popular and useful peripherals

to consider as a family investment. Do not confuse these peripherals with sound systems that many home computers offer as standard equipment. Sound systems are simply speakers and tone or noise generators that make possible various "sound effects" or computer "music."

So we see the shape of a small computer system taking form. The CPU, RAM, and ROM memory constitute the primary elements. Often these components are packaged together with a keyboard and a video screen, as in the Commodore and Radio Shack line of computers. Sometimes the central computer and the memory are packaged with the keyboard only, as in the Apple and the Atari computer. And finally each component may be put in a box of its own, with the keyboard as well as the video in separate modules, as in the IBM Personal Computer.

But regardless of the arrangement, the CPU, RAM (in some quantity), and usually some ROM are present. The keyboard may be one of various styles ranging from those with separate keys like a typewriter, perhaps with a numeric keypad off to one side, to a Mylar printed film input surface, with no separate keys at all. A video display may be built in or added on, or the computer may be adapted to connect to your home television set like the Atari 400, the Commodore VIC-20, or the Radio Shack Color Computer. Some form of mass storage, usually a cassette deck (occasionally modified for this special use), but now more and more commonly a mini-disk drive, must be added to provide off-line memory. And last, a peripheral printer may be attached for hard-copy printouts of relevant information.

We have been through a sea of new terms, concepts, and images. Nobody could be expected to remember or even recognize some of the strange and unnatural language

Figure 7: A Radio Shack Model III showing an integrated keyboard, CRT and floppy disk drive. (Photo courtesy of Radio Shack, a division of Tandy Corporation)

Kids and Computers

that microcomputers have caused to be created. On one side they have usurped some good old names like *memory* and *bit* to refer to some exotic concepts.

On the other side are the neologisms, acronyms, and technical terms to confound us in our attempts to speak about these devices. I have found that one way to get

Figure 8: The keyboard and computer are packaged together. The CRT and two disk drives are in separate units. (Photo courtesy of Apple Computer Inc.)

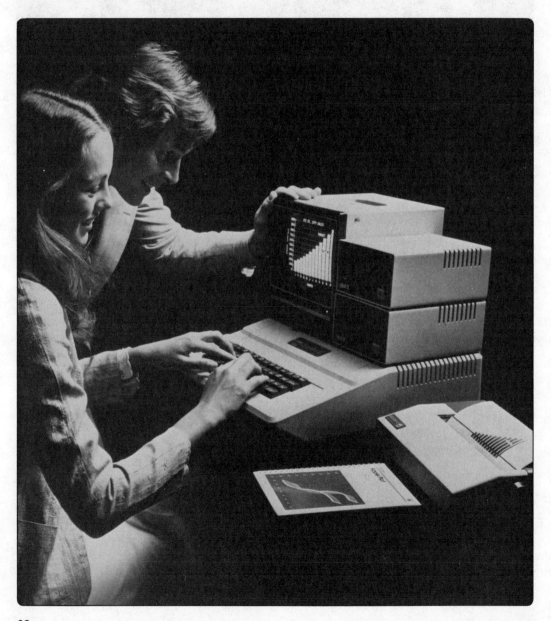

Figure 9: The computer (under the video display). The keyboard and the video display are in separate units. (Photo courtesy of IBM)

Kids and Computers

Figure 10: The Commodore 64 with a typewriter style keyboard and the MAX with a Mylar membrane keyboard. (Photo courtesy Commodore Business Machines Inc.)

straight on what these words and things are is to be quizzed about them. Try the following quiz, and see how well you have retained the tough discussion in this chapter. Answers to the COMPUQUIZZES may be found at the end of the book. Remember 67% correct is a super-score. Anything near 85% qualifies you to apply for admission to our intermediate course, which is coming right up!

Figure 11: The five components of an extended home computer system: the keyboard, the computer, and the video display on the left, a dual disk drive and a printer on the right. (Photo courtesy NEC Home Electronics (U.S.A.) Inc.)

COMPUQUIZ

1. What are the four parts of every computer?

2. What does ROM mean?

3. What is the most common peripheral mass storage system for microcomputers?

4. How many bits are in a byte?

5. What does RAM mean?

6. How much RAM is 32K bytes?

7. The only thing that computers can do is compute. True or false?

8. The most common form of input device for a computer is often called a QWERTY. What is it?

9. The output of a computer can be displayed on a printer or a _____ screen.

That wasn't so bad, was it? You probably remembered more than you thought you would. We will be back to these topics again in Chapter 4, but before I burden you with more technical background, let us address some of the questions that have been asked many times by many concerned parents. Aren't there dangers in computers? Can't they inhibit creativity? Can they hurt your eyes? And possibly most worrying of all, is there any radiation hazard from the display tubes most microcomputers use?

Chapter 3
Keep Out of Reach of Children?

Every technological advance brings hope and fear. Hope comes first: for a tomorrow of smiles, a more comfortable life, opportunity for ourselves and our children. In many cases the hope is realized. Inventions such as the telephone and radio and television have brightened our lives. Other developments have brought implications and potential consequences we do not yet comprehend. We cannot be sure what the result of space flight will be. Perhaps we will populate the universe. Perhaps we will find those who already do. But regardless of the advance publicity, technology is always a coin toss. Sometimes it is possible to anticipate the unwelcome consequences of new ventures. At other times, the consequences sneak up on us to be noticed only when, for some, it may be too late.

Atomic energy is an example of this complicated kind. The technological promise was an energy source that would be too cheap to meter. Electric power would be ours in endless and pollution-free abundance. Those of us who remembered the tall, smoking stacks of the coal-fired electric power plants waited with joy for these new marvels. This potential peaceful use of atomic energy represented to some a justification for the terrible form in which the atomic age made its

debut. Although to some extent the promise was fulfilled, the facts of atomic waste, accidents and their consequences, and the enormous economic costs have dimmed its brightness for the future.

Do computers also present such potential dangers? The computer's entry into our world has been heralded as the cornerstone for a new order. Computers will, in the words of futurists and others who like to guess about tomorrow, make all our lives simpler and more livable. The reasons for this expectation are clear and compelling. Most of our lives are spent in the arrangement and rearrangement of information. We may not always notice this, so perhaps an example will clarify the idea. We have to shop for food: That means we have to check the stock in the larder, make a list of items to be replaced, travel to the store or stores, select the items, review their costs, pay for them or charge them to an account, return home to await delivery, or else tote things home ourselves.

Consider now the computerization of this task. With a computer terminal in our house, we call up the information about our supplies of food, condiments, and household necessities. The machine not only displays what we have in stock, it suggests, on the basis of our rate of use, which items, although still in good supply, should be ordered now and which skipped until a later time. It then prints out a shopping list that simultaneously guarantees that we will not run out of something essential (we have told the computer at start-up what these essentials are) and yet does not overspend our food budget for more stock than is really needed.

Now we touch a few keys to call up prices and brands from various stores. By tapping out our wants, we place orders with several vendors, based on the computer's cross-check of prices, adjusted to allow for preferences for different brands. Our bank account is debited, and the appropriate amount is credited to each vendor. At each store a computer prints out our order with our name, address, and requested delivery time. At the appointed hour the goods ordered arrive. Before they do, the computer prints out our current financial statement, adjusted for our recent purchases. It then reorganizes the distribution of our credit balance to take advantage of local fluctuations in interest rates for the various accounts that hold our reserves. After revising these savings distributions, the machine prints out our next quarter's budget so that we can decide where to spend our summer vacation.

Splendid or scary, these capabilities are available now and could be implemented within a decade. It sounds terrific, you say; but notice that all this information that you live by and with will be stored in some instrinsically public file. No amount of coding and passwords can keep others out of your business for long. You must depend on the prudence and honesty of the institutions that store and use your data. This example, of course, avoided any discussion of information that, in principle, could or should not be made public. But each one of us depends for his or her

psychic independence on some stock of private knowledge. And indeed, the most common current fear of computerizing our lives is the potential for this loss of privacy. Whether such a loss represents a cost that is compensated for by other benefits is a complicated decision that we must make eventually, a decision that will have an impact on both our private and our public lives.

The example just described failed to mention one important and onerous aspect of computerizing one's household. The data and information that the computer used to help us shop did not grow there. It was inserted from a keyboard by someone who had to type in all the relevant facts. This inputting of personal household information and other data represents a large and complicated effort that must not be underestimated. To evaluate intelligently what you hear about computers and the new world, you must consider the amount of time you spend to start up the system. It is not clear that you will have, or even be able to acquire in a reasonable period, the necessary skills to do this job yourself. This means that the age of computers will open new kinds of professional opportunities for the development of useful computer applications. It also means that the service costs may and probably will be higher than the cost of the hardware.

Let us close our discussion of this topic by making one final point about the security of personal information in computer networks. The information stored in a computer is usually located physically on magnetic tape or disk. In the world of little computers such mass storage systems are often inside the computer's case or in a small box next to the keyboard and screen. This means that for personal computers the problem of security does not arise because the information is stored in a device that remains in your physical possession. Automatic and up-to-date processing of, say, your bank balance cannot be realized without some telephone line connection, but with a microcomputer you control the trade-offs by making (relatively) public only what information you choose.

If the dangers of computers are entirely of the philosophical nature described, perhaps as home appliances they are adequately benign. But these days, when we buy household appliances, we often want and need some guarantee of our physical safety. Consider, for example, that the U.S. government licenses manufacturers of microwave ovens. This is because radar ovens may emit stray radiation if they are not properly sealed when their access door is closed. Television sets, especially color television receivers, may also emit radiation that, over long periods

of time if you sit too close, could expose you to radiation levels that may be unhealthy. What about computers? We can address the question from two directions. First, what about current machines? Second, what about the computers of the future?

There are two styles of machines that are now available for home use. One type has a video screen built into or onto the basic unit. The best example of such a unitized microcomputer is the PET® by Commodore Business Machines, Inc. Figure 12 shows how the PET® looks. Radio Shack has also introduced a machine, the TRS-80 Model III, that combines the video screen and the keyboard into a single unit. The Radio Shack TRS-80 Model III is shown in Figure 7. Both of these excellent computers emit about as much radiation as a 12-inch black-and-white TV. This is the case even though

Figure 12: The Commodore PET®, another integrated home computer. Note especially the separate numeric key board on the right. (Photo courtesy of Commodore Business Machines Inc.)

the PET® has green letters on a black screen, whereas the TRS-80 has white letters on a black screen.

The bulk of the evidence is that exposure to such screens, even at distances as close as 12 inches, does not measurably increase a person's radiation load, that is, the level of radiation exposure above the background level. Naturally, duration of exposure is the most relevant measure, and therefore the notion that radiation danger from these machines is minimal is based on home use for perhaps 2 to 4 hours per day. In the work environment, where exposure durations can climb to 8 or more hours per day, the extra radiation load on a person may, at most, approximate the equivalent of an extra dental X ray every five years.

One aspect of these questions that we know little or nothing about concerns the possible effects of even such minute radiation levels on children as compared to adults. Although I have been unable to find data on such a differential, it is obvious that children will have a longer exposure opportunity than will adults. Although this may suggest that care be exercised in terms of total lifetime exposure, new display technologies will undoubtedly alter these total levels.

There is one problem of a less serious nature that may be attributable to sitting close to the video display for long periods of time. You may have noticed that when you get near a TV screen you can "feel" the presence of static electricity. The electric charge generated by the voltages of the beam of the video tube can also induce a static charge onto parts of your body. The result of being "charged up" is that, just as bits of paper and dust cling to a charged hair comb, dust in the air may cling to your hands and face. Some video terminal operators, especially women

who wear makeup, have complained that the static charge can cause dust to cake onto their faces and possibly cause a skin rash. However, the studies that reported these effects were not controlled adequately for possible similar effects due to office carpeting and other sources of ionization in the work place.

Machines such as the Apple II Plus, the IBM Personal Computer, and the Atari have separate video screens, as shown in Figure 13. If the screen used with these machines is a black-and-white TV or a monochromatic video monitor, the previous comments on radiation and static electricity apply. But because these CRTs are only connected to the keyboard by a cable, the screen can be placed further away from you without making the computer inconvenient to use. This means that exposure to any radiation emitted by the tube can be reduced by increasing your distance from it. The relationship of distance to exposure follows the inverse square law. Doubling distance reduces the total cumulative dosage by four. That is, all other things being equal, at twice the distance from the screen you will receive one quarter as much radiation.

On the other hand, if a color monitor or a color TV is used with these machines, the radiation levels at distances that are comfortable for routine computer use (say from 15 inches to 30 inches) may be considerably higher than those previously described. I would avoid operating a microcomputer with a color TV or color monitor as the primary display device. Color TV sets can emit radiation which at very short distances and over long periods may expose you to radiation dosage levels a prudent person might want to avoid. On the other hand, if the computer were used to show graphics or game displays, where the machine was at normal TV viewing

Figure 13: The IBM Personal Computer separates the keyboard from the video display. (Photo courtesy of IBM)

distance, I would have no more concern than I do about color TV in my home. In a work environment I would avoid color TV displays altogether at the individual work station. At greater viewing distances, e.g., across a room or on a distant wall, I would have no concern.

The main point, then, is that radiation levels depend on distance from the source. Levels are reduced by four if the viewing distance from the screen, say 12 inches, is increased by two, to 24 inches, and further reduced by sixteen if the distance is increased to 48 inches.

To summarize these comments and cautions: The radiation problem depends on a mixture of distance, intensity, and time. We want to minimize the total cumulative dosage. Eight hours a day at a distance of 12 inches exposes us to four times the total cumulative radiation we would receive if the screen was moved to 24 inches. Alternatively, two hours a day at 12 inches exposes us to the same radiation we would receive from a screen at 24 inches in 8 hours. But none of these

exposure levels is very high, because four times very little is still very little. With color video, however, the problem may change. Radiation levels from a color video screen can be twelve to twenty times higher than from a black-and-white (or green) screen. Finally, static electricity induced onto your skin from the charge on the face of the video tube may require extra washing to remove the dust you may attract.

A review of these considerations has led several European countries to require computer manufacturers to separate the video screen from the computer as the Apple and Atari do. This allows the user to adjust the distance to the screen without having to reach too far for the keyboard. But having separate boxes, with their associated cables and connector plugs, in my opinion generates a cost in terms of simplicity and reliability. In fact, in The Children's Computer School classrooms, I minimize the use of computers that do not have integral screens. This is because risk of damage to a child from the implosion of a video tube inadvertently pushed off the keyboard or even of a smashed toe, is a quantitatively and qualitatively greater danger than the minute radiation levels produced by these devices.

Future developments will almost certainly make all this discussion academic. I anticipate that very shortly large liquid-crystal screens (the kind that are commonly used in digital watches), gas-discharge screens, and vacuum-fluorescent screens will completely replace video tubes as the display device for home computers. When this new display technology is established, questions will be directed toward problems of eyestrain rather than radiation. This possible problem, though of less consequence, may perhaps create more difficulties in the use of these machines than can now be anticipated.

Indeed, radiation aside, one of the main complaints that people express about the use of computers, or any CRT-type termi-

nals for that matter, is eyestrain and other feelings of fatigue and discomfort. As far as eyestrain is concerned, there is probably good reason to believe that the use of video terminals, or microcomputers that are modeled on them, does lead to visual fatigue. This complaint is most common among people who use these machines 30 to 40 hours a week. But different machines are more or less pleasant to use, even at the moderate levels of home or hobby use, depending on certain factors.

You should understand that the letters and numbers that you see on the screen of a microcomputer are composed of tiny dots that form the letters. Figure 14 shows how a rectangular collection of tiny dots can be lit up to form any of the letters and numbers that can be shown on the screen. Some machines use smaller dots and more of them for each letter. Others use fewer and larger dots to form the letters. Other considerations being equal,

Figure 14: A screen display of an arithmetic game. The numbers and letters are made of little squares called picture elements or pixels.

the display with more dots per letter is always more comfortable to use and (usually but not always) more expensive to buy. The problem is that the dots serve as a stimulus on which your eye focuses, and yet the letters are easier to read if you can defocus and "smear" the dots. This may require continuous visual adjustments that induce the sensations of strain. The solution to this problem is to compare carefully the CRT displays of competitive machines, and be sure to select one that you find reasonably comfortable to use.

There is a large difference in appearance of things seen by reflected light, such as print on paper, or most of the real objects in the world around us, and things that emit light energy, like a TV picture. Usually people prefer to dim the surrounding light when they are watching light-emitting displays like TVs and to turn on the lights when they look at reflected-light images. When looking at objects by reflected light, it is easy to transfer from looking at the object of interest to other things around you. But when you are watching light emitted from a display, looking away results in a sudden switch from light to dark. This switching of the average intensity of the light to which the eyes are exposed results in a form of fatigue, or eyestrain, that often accompanies use of video displays.

However, if the regular room light is cleverly adjusted to illuminate the area surrounding the screen but still permits high contrast in the light coming from the video display, the problem does not arise. It is the difficulty of arranging these conditions that leads people to complain about the use of such displays. There is no doubt that operators, especially if they must work for extended periods of time without a break, experience annoying ocular sensations. You should recognize that these problems are neither permanent nor necessary. The solution to them simply requires careful attention to the visual world that surrounds the working visual field. The visual problems are compounded by failure to arrange seating and table height to prevent muscular strain and by poor postural adjustments. These difficulties are increased for those who wear bifocal glasses and especially when we share the machine with our children, whose size and visual capabilities are different from ours.

When you get your own microcomputer home, consider how you plan to use it before selecting a location to set it up. Remember that you will probably change your patterns of use as you become acquainted with the power of the computer. Also remember that your children may want to work on the machine when you are doing other things. After a computer work place has been found, you should attend to two problems in arranging the lights near it. First, avoid having any light shining on the screen or reflecting into your eyes when you sit at the keyboard. Be sure to have your children check out this glare problem, because they often sit lower in relation to the tube or work at a different angle to the screen than an adult. Second, be sure to have enough indirect light near the machine to properly light the keyboard. I have arranged this at my own computer work station by using an architect's flexible-arm lamp with the light pointed at the white ceiling above the computer. This reflects enough light down onto the keyboard without causing any light to shine on the face of the CRT screen.

Sometimes experts present arguments that suggest that variations of the letter color or the background color of these screens may reduce annoyance from glare or surrounding lighting. Various colors have been suggested and used for the pictures or letters shown on a screen. At this point in history three alternative color combinations appear to be in the running. Most video display tubes—which are often called CRTs, short for *cathode-ray tubes*—used with computers show letters and graphics as either white on black or dark gray, or green on black or gray. Although the Federal Aviation Administration came down in favor of green on black based on their research with air traffic controllers using radar screens, either form seems comfortable to most people. I prefer white on black even though I use a machine that has a green screen. I like other features of my computer and consider the screen color to be less important than things like the "feel" of the keyboard. A third, orange-colored phosphor is being used now on several new microcomputers.

One company makes display screens for their expensive word processors with a lighted background (white); the letters or graphics are traced in black. Other displays use this *reverse video* mode with green phosphors. This black on white arrangement is designed to be more like the image we are used to seeing in print or typing on paper. In fact, the familiarity of this arrangement is surely less important than its brightness, which helps it compete more easily with surrounding bright objects. This probably contributes to easier use at a work station in brightly lighted spaces. However, for routine computer use most people accept the usual display consisting of bright letters on a dark background.

A display in which letters are of one color and the background is a color other than black (or gray) is normally achieved by using a color TV or color monitor as the computer display screen. Although this generates a temporary novelty that may be of interest or importance for specific tasks,

the need to use a device with higher than necessary radiation levels seems to make that advantage a poor trade-off.

We started the chapter with broad philosophic concerns about dangers inherent in computers and their use. Those dangers, although real and important, are less likely to stand in the way of the expansion of this technology than other considerations that might show up at the personal level. A question that every parent should ask about computers and their use is what they do to a child's ability to think and reason. Do computers tend to suppress creativity? Do they lead to laziness in thinking? Do they interfere with other activities? Our experience, which spans the teaching of several thousand students to program computers, suggests the following answers to these questions:

1. Successfully programming a computer depends on critical thinking and problem solving.

2. Computer programming enhances existing creativity, particularly in problem solving and rational thinking.

3. Working at a computer is addictive, especially if the student is good at it. The curriculum must be arranged to prevent total absorption in computer activities.

4. Computer operations are not mathematical in form. Children who have difficulty with mathematics are often able to program exceptionally well.

5. If anything, girls seem more able in learning to program than boys.

What may be a more subtle question is often raised by parents, especially those with exceptionally able children who excel in the arts or other creative activities. This is the question of whether computer skills, although effective in the aid of rational thinking, may not stultify the artistically creative child. Do computers instill a rigidity of thinking that de-emphasizes other important modes of thought? Even more important is the feeling of some parents that the computer skill may de-emphasize social values and indeed the very human qualities that are the root and being of civilization. May we become a race of robots, able only to program our way through the mundane existence of our material world? Perhaps programming computers really results in programming ourselves to serve the computer master.

These are awesome issues. More fearful even than a revolt of the robots is conversion by the robots. If these machines can change our human nature, then questions of loss of privacy, or other damaging consequences of computer use, fall away to nothing. The only plausible answer to questions of this kind is to cite the resiliency of the human spirit. Once the instrinsic properties of these machines are understood, any supernatural power they may seem to wield vanishes. Ignorance of the workings of things is a generator of anxiety and concern. When a child and his or her parents recognize that these devices are nothing more than an inert though complex system of interrelated parts—a complicated machine—there is no basis for anxiety. Most kids play with computers, in the same sense that they play with a puppy or a kitten. As to creative activities, we have students who enjoy both computer programming and playing the flute, and in our word-processing courses for high school and college students, the majority want the skill and the machines for creative writing.

Of course there are some children who are lured into unwholesome behavior. They spend hours of their time at home playing computer games that have no

intrinsic redeeming value. We have found that the best and easiest way to cope with this wasteful activity is to require a program analysis of the game. This results in the child's playing the game for a genuinely intellectual purpose. Some kids who once spent much of their time playing games have now turned to writing games. Game programming is one of the most sophisticated forms of program creation. Often the best game programmers become junior teachers of other children. They can usually clear up another child's confusion about some complicated coding faster than an adult teacher. We aim for such redirection of effort whenever problems with computer misuse arise. They are not always readily solvable however, in which case we depend on parental sanctions. But as our experience and skill develop, we may redirect more of these avid computerists into channels of lasting value.

The toughest cases are the rare kids who direct all of their interest and activity into computers. These are the "hackers," who can be found at most large computer installations, usually at the college level. Their interest, if it is contained and directed, can be and often is the basis for enormous professional success. But some of these youngsters become addicted to the machine for its own sake. Their work in other areas suffers. Their social life deteriorates, and they become so entranced that they can hardly be pulled away from the machine. I know of no real answer to this problem, although parental interest and guidance may help. At the very least it will demonstrate your concern as you illuminate the consequences of such single-minded pursuits.

So all things considered, as yet there appear to be no cognitive dangers associated with computer skills. Even among the hackers the central problem is usually social. Obviously, I am talking about computer programming taught and practiced under the watchful eye of teachers who are specially trained to teach children about computers. Such training requires curricular organization that defends the child from experiences with a computer that are self-defeating. An early example of such negative experience arose when our first curricular outlines were tried on my own children.

First, you must know that computers distinguish between the names they give to storage locations for numbers and for words. In all the teaching manuals for computer programming at that time, students were introduced to the number game first. I tried it this way too and almost failed to communicate with my second daughter, Gabrielle. She did not want to get involved with a machine that talked numbers. I learned very quickly that we had started on the wrong foot. To this day I find in many school programs a failure to appreciate the importance of curricular structure as it determines student interest and

involvement, at least in computer literacy. Several educators have proposed to me that only older children can successfully absorb computer education. These proposals are based on their view that children must use the computer for the purposes professionals do, and that usually means mathematical purposes.

We know from our success at The Children's Computer School with more than two thousand students that curricula without dependence on numbers can be devised that can be used in a classroom with children as young as 7. Eventually, as the child matures and broadens his or her knowledge and skill in mathematics, we introduce the programming base for dealing with these concepts. This valuable experience should serve to support your continuing interest in your child's (and your own!) studies and investigations of computers and computer programming. In the meantime, there is no need to be anxious. As we shall see, computers are often better with words than they are with arithmetic.

Chapter 4
The Microcomputer's Parts

What is a computer? I guess it depends on which movie you've seen lately. Sometimes it's flashing lights and tape-recording machines. Other times it may be a typewriter terminal with yards of paper streaming out of it. Occasionally, it is a video tube or screen on which pictures or letters and numbers appear. In point of fact, any or all of these images may be a plausible notion of a computer. In order to think about things we need such images, or words that blend into images, to give structure to our thoughts. But the best way to think about things, as we all know, is not by appearance as such, but by their fundamental parts or functions. If you understand the purpose of a part of something, the "thing" takes on an aura of understandability. Most of our school time is spent just trying to get hold of the purpose or function of parts of complicated things, ideas, or systems.

A computer, like any other complicated device, is made up of parts. But just as we do not need to know about every part of every other device we use, it is not necessary to know about every part of a computer. Indeed as we saw in Chapter 2, every computer has only four main components.

1. the input system—usually a keyboard

2. the output system—usually a video tube

3. the central processor

4. the memory

Let us review these parts again to be sure we know their purpose and function.

The computer requires that information or instructions from the user be fed into it. This *inputting* of information and instruction is served by the input system. The keyboard of the input system lets us enter letters and numbers that the computer uses to do what we want done. In a very real sense the input system of a computer is no different from the light switch on the wall that "inputs" our desire that the lights go on. The wall switch does only two things (it is a truly binary digital device). Because its "central processor" is so exceedingly simple, it can only distinguish two states of being—ON or OFF. The computer keyboard permits us to enter a pattern of switch (keystroke) settings so that the computer can do one thing for one pattern and something else for other patterns.

While we are on the topic of entering information and instructions, let's talk about the name of this object of our study. As you will recall, the name *computer* reflects the fact that early machines of this kind were used primarily to make numerical calculations. Today, the main purpose of the machine is to *massage* information from one form into another. The machine is really an *information processor* but the name doesn't reflect this important fact. Many people unfamiliar with computers are put off by the name of the machine, which makes it sound like "numbers and math," but we should not be misled. The computer is only occasionally called on by us actually to compute, (though in daily use it may compute wildly on the inside to make our information processing simple on the outside). This internal computation may be the reason the name *computer* sticks. However, for our practical purposes computation is only a part, and a small one, of that for which we can use an information processor.

This point brings up another slight confusion that I often see, usually among businessmen and -women. When computers were adapted by their internally stored programs to produce typed letters, they were sold under the name *word processors*. These machines could be used to enter text from a keyboard and then do various things like storing, searching, replacing, moving, or duplicating the text. Many people thought that these machines were some special breed of cat. They were not. They were merely computers with specific programs (internal instructions) in them. They could serve to do other things just as well, and now the manufacturers of these devices have revealed this truth to us. Almost every word processor can now load and execute other programs besides the one for which it was designed in the first place. Again we see that computers are really devices for dealing with information, whether that information be words, numbers, or even pictures, graphs, or charts.

The *output* system is the part of a computer that turns its internal machinations into something we humans can deal with. Usually, the output system generates displays of information or data in the form of lists, graphs, charts, text, or tables. This information may range from such things as the single number that represents our October bank balance to the pictorial display of the caverns and tunnels of a game of Dungeons and Dragons. Either may be displayed by the same kind of output device. However, if the output system is a printing device, the game moves along slowly. For such fast-moving, dynamic outputs we usually prefer a video screen (a CRT). On the other hand, if we want to prepare our yearly income tax, it would be preferable to output our data and calculations to a printing device that would print out our tax form.

Output systems of both kinds—printers and CRTs—are in common use. Usually, a microcomputer either comes with a CRT built in or on it, as for example the Commodore PET®, or it attaches to a television set or monitor and uses that video tube as its CRT. Machines like the Atari and the Apple are of this type. Printers for use with microcomputers are considered to be a secondary and less preferred form of output. They are also intrinsically more expensive and harder to keep in repair than CRTs. As a result, the owner of a microcomputer who wants output data printed out buys a separate printer.

A computer *printer* is like a typewriter without keys. Many of them print out computer materials on special paper. Sometimes the paper is merely perforated on each side so that the printer can advance it without slipping a line. Other machines require a special chemically prepared paper that is printed on, not by type and an inked ribbon, but by heat or electric discharge. Such paper can be expensive to use if a lot of output is generated. The most convenient printers are those that use plain paper, either with side perforations for continuous printing, or single sheets. These printers often use a printing method called *dot matrix printing.* Dot matrix printing consists of tiny dots arranged in the form of letters. Each letter is really a selection of dots from some standard *block* of possible dots that may look like

Figure 15. Notice that the dots in this 5 wide × 9 high matrix can be filled to make any letter or number. A 5 × 9 matrix like this can accommodate *descenders,* the parts of the letters g, j, p, q, and y, that go below the line. If the dot matrix is smaller, as it is in less expensive dot matrix printers, such descenders cannot be printed. In continuous text, such as letters or other documents, the absence of descenders is annoying to the reader.

Figure 15: The 5 × 9 character block that accommodates upper- and lower-case characters with descenders.

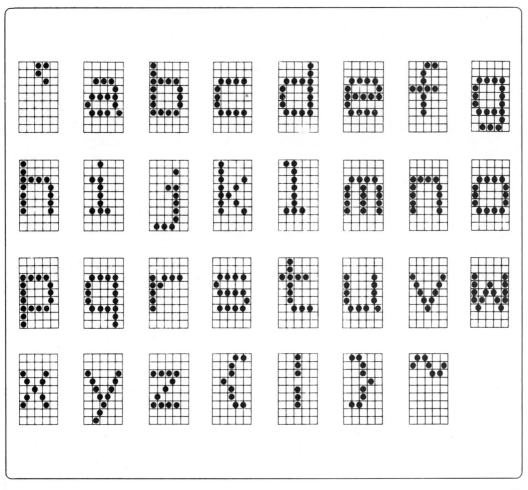

Kids and Computers

There are other kinds of printers available that connect to microcomputers as "add-on" or peripheral devices. One large class of currently desirable printers are called *daisy wheel printers*. Figure 16 shows such a daisy wheel printer, and Figure 17 illustrates the daisy wheel itself. This machine works by rotating the daisy wheel until the correct letter is lined up at the impact point. Then a small hammer controlled by an electrical impulse strikes the flexible letter *petal* of the daisy wheel, pressing it against an inked ribbon onto the paper to form the printed letter. These printers make print much like a standard typewriter. Consequently, they are often called *letter-quality printers* to distinguish their work from dot matrix printers.

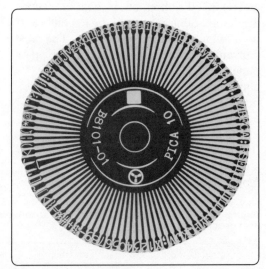

Figure 17: Daisy wheel.

Figure 16: A daisy wheel letter-quality printer.

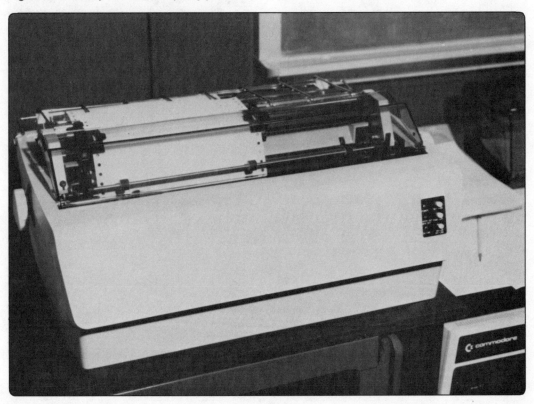

The best and most expensive letter-quality printers operate at a top speed of about 60 letters per second, which is quite fast. The least expensive dot matrix printer without descenders prints even faster at about 80 characters per second. The least expensive letter-quality printer currently costs about twice as much as the least expensive dot matrix printer, and this expensive daisy wheel prints at one-eighth the speed of the dot matrix. The advantages of dot matrix printing appear overwhelming. Then why are letter-quality daisy wheel printers sold? The fact is that aesthetics may be an overriding consideration in many, and perhaps most, commercial applications. There is no question that daisy wheel printing looks neat and professional. On the other hand, this judgment may be the result of past experience and expectations. As dot matrix printed material becomes more common, its aesthetic disadvantages may disappear. Already, some publishers are accepting authors' manuscripts printed on dot matrix machines. However, dot matrix printing, even with descenders, is harder to read for long periods of time than is letter-quality print. The reason for this is again probably the difficulty the eye has when trying to focus on letters while in fact focusing on individual dots. Newer developments in this area are on the way, and like video screens, the dot matrix printer may soon be a thing of the past.

Speech synthesizers and speech recognizers were mentioned in Chapter 2 as input-output systems of growing sophistication and popularity. Like the video screen, the output of a speech synthesizer is transient and ephemeral. Consequently, the value of such output is most obvious during interactive use of the microcomputer, for example in educational or certain information processing modes. When used for these purposes speech output may be useful to warn of errors or confusions in the use of the machine. For example, spoken words can be used effectively to correct technical and syntactical mistakes when the microcomputer is used for word processing or for teaching. Imagine your computer saying, "Please reenter that answer, I don't recognize the word after 'tangent.'"

Regardless of the kind of printing or speaking devices that you may attach as peripheral outputs to a microcomputer, the primary output system of every microcomputer will continue to be a visual electronic display such as a video screen, or its equivalent. As was pointed out in the previous chapter, one concern that people have about the safety of computers rests on the perceived universal presence of the CRT and its potential radiation problems. There will certainly be changes and improvements such as the flat-screen displays mentioned in Chapter 3 that will replace the CRT, but for the moment the CRT is the de facto standard of the industry.

CRT displays come in two forms: (1) dedicated monitors built into or added onto the computer and (2) television sets coupled to the computer. First of all, let us distinguish between monitors and TVs. Television sets have the ability to receive TV signals and convert them into pictures on a screen. Monitors are not able to receive TV pictures off the air. They do not contain a *tuning section* and thus cannot select channels to display program material. They are picture tubes only. Such monitors, however, because they do not have to serve as TV receivers, often can display finer detail on their screens. This is important if text material composed of letters and numbers is going to be displayed. Therefore, one generally gets a better image of letters and numbers using a monitor, whether integral or separate, rather than a TV receiver.

Even when a monitor is used, microcomputers vary in their ability to generate fine enough detail to "print" lots of letters on the CRT. For many purposes the CRT can generate enough information for routine use if the screen surface is divided into about 1000 (imaginary) blocks, or *pixels.* The word *pixel,* short for PIXcture ELement, refers to the number of discrete places on the screen that a single letter or number can occupy. One thousand pixels can be arranged into 25 rows of lines of 40 characters or columns. The Apple, the Atari, and the PET® all use a 1000-pixel display. The Radio Shack TRS-80 Model III distributes its 1024 pixels in 16 rows of 64 columns. Some machines, including the Commodore CBM 8000 series, the TRS-80 Model II, and modified Apple IIs can display about 2000 characters. These displays use 24 or 25 rows of 80 characters each. The advantage of this increase in screen resolution is that text on the screen can show line lengths that correspond to lines typed on a page of standard 8½ inch × 11 inch paper. Because the screen height of most CRTs still limits the display to 25 lines, less than half a page of single-spaced material can be seen at one time. This limitation is usually overcome by *vertical scrolling.* This means that the screen page acts like a movable window covering the real page; this window can move up and down to reveal any 25 lines of the output we may care to see. In some educational programs scrolling is used to advance to new material or return to old material, depending on the success of the student. All microcomputers can scroll the screen display under program control. Many machines dedicate a special block of

RAM memory to the screen and use this memory to accomplish the scrolling of several screens full of information.

Before we discuss the central processing unit, we should recognize that the input and output features of a microcomputer are designed to work together. This means that the output, whether screen or printer, commonly "echoes" the input keystrokes so that the user can see immediately if the correct key was pressed, that is, the computer outputs every input (unless it is programmed not to) so that errors of input can be noted and corrected as they are made. The nature of such error correction, called *editing,* depends on the computer and how it works. Some machines require that the corrections be caught and made immediately, or else revised at a later time in special ways. Others permit revisions at special screen locations any time after entry of data or programs. Still others permit you to move a *cursor,* a small block of light, or an underline character, that tells where the input will print on the screen, and then let you type over, add, or delete input information at the cursor location. In whatever way the editing is done, it is a necessary feature of every computer, for if there is one thing about using a computer that is as certain as sunset, it is that you are bound to make mistakes during input. The best part about it is that only you and the computer know, and the computer is certain to tell you (nicely, mind you!) so that the mistakes can be fixed.

The compu*to*r, the part that computes, as distinct from the compu*te*r, the machine itself, is housed in a large-scale integrated circuit (LSI) called the *central processor.* These LSI chips are the heart of the computer. The central processor is where all input information passes on its way to various other internal parts of the machine; it is also the point at which control of the output system is maintained. This central processor is shown in one of its various forms in Figure 18. The little legs that make it look like a centipede are the electrical connectors that connect the circuit itself with the rest of the machine. The LSI circuit is shown in Figure 19 in an enlarged view that shows the connections between its various parts. The actual size of the LSI circuit is about ¼-inch square. That is why it is buried in plastic so that people with human-sized fingers can plug it into the circuit boards that make up the interior of the computer. Figure 20 shows such a computer circuit board and the various LSI chips that are plugged into it.

The central processor performs only a few primitive logical functions, but it

Figure 18: A chip mounted inside its plastic carrier. (Photo courtesy of Intel Corporation)

Figure 19: The complex circuit of the chip is shown at the bottom of the illustration. (Photo courtesy of Intel Corporation)

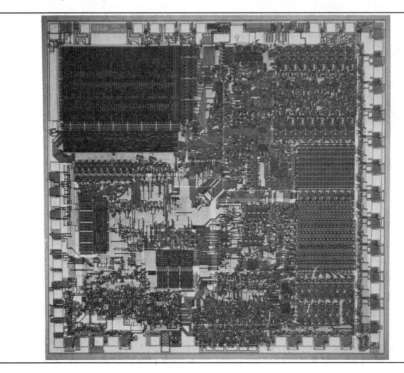

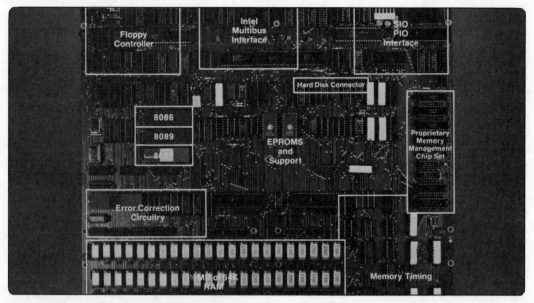

Figure 20: A circuit board containing a gaggle of chips. The CPU is on the left center numbered 8086. (Photo courtesy of Cromenco Inc.)

performs them at great speed, from perhaps 1 to 6 million times per second. What Alan Turing had proved in his famous paper of 1937 was that a few logical functions, if done often enough, serve to permit more complex logic such as *equal to, greater than, if . . . then,* and *branch to.* When a machine is able to perform these and other logical operations, then anything one can talk about without internal contradictions can be done by the machine. But just because the central processor can process 4 million operations per second does not mean that it alone can compute. The information to be processed has to come from somewhere; it cannot all be stored in the central processor. Of course it comes from input from the keyboard, but it has to be stored somewhere in the computer to let the CPU get to it fast and often. For this the computer depends on other LSI chips on its circuit board. These chips contain the computer's memory. In

fact, they retain the instructions about how the CPU should act, as well as the information and data that are to be acted upon or processed.

The connections between the various chips on the computer circuit board, and the internal structure of the CPU represents what the computer engineer and designer call the *computer architecture.* First of all, the CPU is linked to the rest of the computer memory by what are called *buses.* There are three primary kinds: (1) the address bus, (2) the control bus, and (3) the data bus. These buses are shown as the large arrows in Figure 21. The address bus is used to carry the location of a memory box in RAM or ROM from the CPU to the memory, where the control bus directs whether information is to be entered or copied. The information, either program commands or data, for they are intrinsically interchangeable, flow along the data bus either to or from the CPU. For example, if the computer must write an instruction to its memory, that datum is placed on the data bus, with its address on the address bus, and a command on the control bus that instructs the computer to write the data to the appropriate memory location.

The computer memory in most microcomputers is divided, as we have pointed out, into two kinds: read-only memory (ROM) and random access memory (RAM). ROM belongs to the computer in a way that RAM does not. ROM contains special instructions and programs written in the CPU's primitive language (called *machine language*). These instructions may include procedures to permit the CPU to understand other kinds of instruction that you may input. These instructional programs that you input may be written in

a language that is easier for you to understand, like BASIC, rather than the machine language that the CPU loves. So the ROM often contains a system that translates your easily understood English-like BASIC instructions into machine-language instructions. In addition the ROM usually contains "housekeeping" instructions for the CPU, telling the CPU where various kinds of information will be stored away and how to get that information and use it. All this stuff is commonly called the *operating system* of the computer. If the operating system is stored in ROM, then from the moment the machine is turned on, the operating system is available to the CPU to use. For this reason an operating system stored in ROM, or any ROM-based information the computer uses to perform its work, is called *firmware*.

Figure 21: The architecture and the three main buses of the CPU and the memory.

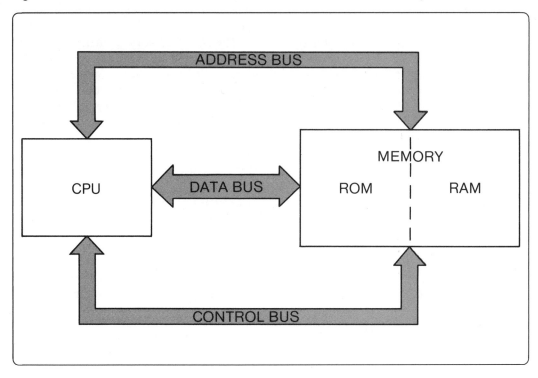

Kids and Computers

Sometimes the operating system is not stored in ROM but has to be sent into the RAM memory of the computer from storage outside the computer, say from a tape or disk storage system. In these computers, the operating system is loaded as the first project after the computer is turned on. Some computers contain a small ROM that may automatically run a short program to load the operating system. This program, a *bootstrap* program, may be the only firmware in the computer. When it runs to boot-up the operating system, a large segment of RAM is reserved and is not used for your programs or data. Machines like the Osborne 1 use such a system. Some machines have a hybrid operating system. A small but adequate operating system is stored in ROM, but bootstrap programs are also available to load enhancements of the operating system into RAM for more advanced program handling. The Apple II operates in this hybrid mode.

Finally, there are microcomputer systems in which additional ROM can be plugged into the circuit board or into a special accessory cartridge. These machines can then be upgraded by the addition of this extra memory that contains sophisticated programs for doing special kinds of commands and operations. A good example of a system of this kind is the Hewlett-Packard HP-85 which sports a ROM *drawer* into which six additional ROMs can be inserted. Some of these memories are used to increase the number of different commands the programmer can use to write programs. Others may serve to permit the easy attachment and operation of peripheral devices such as graphics plotters for drawing diagrams and figures with computer precision. The most popular use of add-on, or perhaps we should call it plug-in ROM, is to store programs for games and other popular and widely distributed computer programs. But we will have more to say about this later.

Understanding the facts in the previous paragraphs may help you avoid confusion about memory size when comparing computers. Usually the memory of importance to the purchaser is the RAM available for program and data storage. Where a machine requires that an operating system be booted into RAM, the fact that the RAM size seems large is often an illusion. If the machine has 48K of RAM but requires 28K for the operating system and the programming language, the usable RAM is 20K. This is quite a bit less than a microcomputer system with 32K of usable RAM, with its operating system completely contained in ROM. So when you compare a machine with 48K of RAM with one that has 32K you must determine how much of the RAM in each of the machines will be used in the "overhead" of the computer's operations.

The RAM memory, as mentioned previously, should be called read-write memory and has an important property not shared by ROM. When the computer is turned off, the RAM forgets all it had stored. It is a volatile memory that depends on a steady supply of electricity to keep its information from fading. Although RAM has this apparent defect, this ability means that you can store something in one of its memory cells now and change it later if necessary. Interestingly, when you read the information from a memory cell in RAM, the information is merely copied, not deleted. Memory in RAM is only changed; it is never erased. Obviously, if you change the memory of a RAM location to "nothing," that is pretty close to erased, but notice that it is only changed. The RAM is the part of the computer that contains the user's data and instructions to the computer. Because RAM is volatile, the preceding comment suggests that the computer must either be left on all the time or another way has to be found to preserve your data and instructional programs when the machine is turned off. This, of course, is why the peripheral mass storage system—the cassette tapes and floppy disks mentioned in Chapter 2—are almost a necessity.

The connections between the peripheral devices and the CPU are called *ports.* There are two kinds—input ports and output ports—depending on whether they go to the keyboard or to the screen or printer.

The internal architecture of the CPU is more complicated than the memory registers. The CPU is divided into four parts. The first is a clock that keeps all the operations synchronized. This clock races along at perhaps 4 million beats per second! The next part is the central control circuitry. The third is a unit that performs the logical and arithmetical operations, such as comparing two values or adding two numbers. Finally, the CPU has its own local memory, called *registers,* that it uses for temporary storage. These parts of the CPU are shown schematically in Figure 22.

We have mentioned the term *peripheral* before when we were talking about printers as optional output devices. The main peripheral that every computer needs is not a printer or any other output device. Nor is it some kind of special keyboard or user-oriented input device like a *joystick,* which is a small controller used mostly for games. Every computer worthy of the name

Figure 22: The partitioning of the CPU into its four main parts. Often the clock is physically separated from the rest of the CPU.

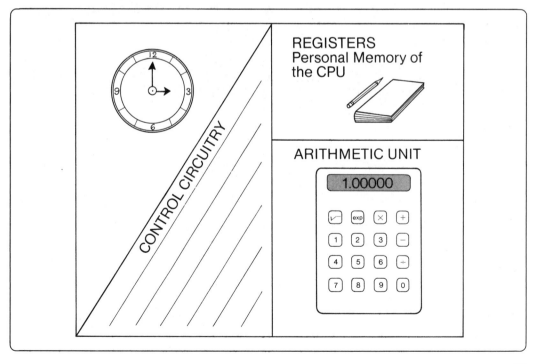

needs a system that the computer can use for both input and output. Such a peripheral is called a *mass storage system.* The point is that if a computer loses all its RAM information when it is turned off, there must be some way to preserve that information in a form that is independent of the RAM. Such a system is a mass storage system. One early form of mass storage used by microcomputers was punched paper-tape devices. Quite soon, however, hobbyists and manufacturers of computer hardware learned to use cassette tape recorders like the one shown in Chapter 2, Figure 5 as a mass storage system.

After all, a cassette tape can remember music, so why not have it remember computer data? No sooner said then done. Every currently available microcomputer has a cassette tape mass storage system that will preserve both the data in RAM and the computer user's program that is also stored in RAM.

Cassette recorders are simple, reliable, and cheap. They are also quite slow when used to store computer information. Consider that a cassette tape might take as long as 6 or 7 minutes to load the RAM of a microcomputer. "Not long," you say. But after a few sessions of waiting for your favorite game program to load into the computer's RAM, you start to wish for a newer mass storage technology—the floppy disk. These storage systems currently come in 3 sizes: 3¼, 5¼, and 8 inches in diameter. The larger disks are most common in office systems used for business and professional computing. However, there is a move

Figure 23: Mini-floppy.

toward the smaller *mini-floppies* or micro-floppies even in larger business computers. There is no intrinsic advantage in the larger disk, except greater storage capacity.

The mini-floppy (sometimes called a *mini-disk,* or *diskette*) is shown in Figure 23; a *disk drive* is shown in Figure 24. The disk itself is a circle of thin Mylar plastic that has been coated with a magnetic film much like the coating on audio- or videotape. It is housed in a square card-board protective cover that contains a slot to expose the magnetic material to the read and write heads in the disk drive. The squareness of the protective cover makes some people wonder why it is called a "disk." The disk, of course, is inside. The disk drive is like a phonograph turn-table that can record and play back computer data and programs on the floppy disk. Because the disk drive is controlled by part of the computer's operating system (sometimes in ROM) it can seek various programs or data that have been recorded on various *tracks* and *sectors* of the disk. These tracks and sectors are kept account of by the disk operating system (DOS) stored in the computer's own memory, either in ROM or in RAM. Some disk drives, part of a group of "intelligent" peripherals, contain their own RAM, ROM, and even a CPU to take care of the DOS. These disk systems do not require the main computer to use part of its own memory for the DOS.

The advantages of floppy disk mass storage systems are twofold. First, the game discussed previously that took 6 or 7 minutes to load from cassette would load from disk in less than 9 seconds.

Figure 24: This single disk drive can store more than 150,000 characters on a single disk. Some units can store as many as 1,000,000 characters on a disk of the same size. (Photo courtesy of Commodore Business Machines Inc.)

Kids and Computers

Second, instead of you searching for the place on the cassette tape where the program was located, the disk directory containing the names and addresses of all the programs and data on the disk, could be sent to your video screen. You would then instruct the computer to *load* the program by entering its name, and in less than 10 seconds the job would be done.

The mass storage peripheral device is always an option when a microcomputer is purchased. If you simply wanted to enter instructions to the computer each time you turned it on, you would not need a mass storage system. For programs that only make your computer process information, mass storage is merely a convenience. Such programs include games or other activities that do not depend on fresh data. But notice that if the program requires data to be entered, such as the checks you wrote this month, to whom they were made out, and whether they were deductible or nondeductible expenses, or the spelling lists of your child's spelling program, then without a mass storage system to preserve the data, it is useless to use the computer for this task. Data that are to be used again by the computer must be stored on a mass storage system that is peripheral to the computer itself. I routinely recommend that parents contemplating purchase of a computer always include at least a simple cassette mass storage system that will operate with the computer. Floppy disks and other enhancements can wait until skill has developed, both in operation and in understanding.

The most technically advanced mass storage peripherals are the *hard* disk drives. These are often called by their informal name: Winchesters. That name comes from the fact that when the IBM Corporation first introduced a small hard disk drive it carried model number 3030, the caliber designation of the classic Winchester .30/.30 lever action rifle. The hard disk has advantages over the floppy disk, but it has disadvantages also. First, it is a sealed unit, in which the information-bearing magnetic surface is protected by the casing from contact with an injurious environment. Particles of dust, tobacco smoke, or a spilled cup of coffee cannot reach the stored information. Second, the amount of information that can be stored on the unit for immediate access is from 10 to 1000 times greater than the information on the most densely packed floppy. Third, the reliability of information retrieval is 10 to 100 times greater than the reliability of a floppy disk.

The disadvantages of the Winchester include price, which at the moment is about five times that of a floppy disk drive. Also, the sealed feature of the unit contrasts with the removable media of the cassette recorder and the floppy disk drive. Once the hard disk is full, something must be erased to permit room for more storage. Finally, whereas you can make a copy of the information on a floppy disk in order to "back up" the information in case of loss or damage, the backup for a hard disk comes at the cost of additional equipment and the need for a removable medium. Currently, hard disks are backed up onto either ½-inch videotape, using a specially modified video recorder, or onto floppy disks just like the ones used as a separate storage medium. It seems clear that the first choice for an advanced mass storage system is a floppy disk drive followed, if the need develops, with a Winchester hard disk.

You will recall that some computers have the option of inserting ROM memory into the existing machine. These ROMs may contain special operating system programs or other programming enhancements. However, there is one type of ROM insert that is quite different from operating system ROMs. These ROMs are usually called *game cartridges.* Some computers, such as the low-cost Atari and the VIC-20, have access holes into which ROM cartridges can be inserted. Such game cartridges are just peripheral mass storage systems. As such they could be replaced by games stored on cassette tape or floppy disks. Many such tape- and disk-based game programs do exist, but the ease of loading and converting your computer to a game-playing machine by using an insertable ROM makes these devices attractive for this special purpose.

I believe that as high-quality programming for educational purposes develops (and it has not shown much quality up to now), such programs may also be ROM based. Indeed, the convenience of ROM-based utility programs is bound to increase, since these devices effectively convert a multipurpose machine into a potentially unique single-purpose system. By adding additional input systems such as light pens, joysticks, and game paddles, the game systems have shown how special-purpose devices can be derived from a general-purpose computer.

Imagine for a moment a library of ROM-based information, perhaps stored on new forms of memory, such as magnetic bubbles or laser-scanned video-type disks. Such a collection could pack the Library of Congress in your living room. When loaded into your microcomputer it would not only provide text material, interactive discussions and lectures, as well as programmed instruction in practical and applied skills, but could interleave this material with standard video images to display movies and entertainment related to the subject of your interest.

Before we are carried away with these flights of the future, let us consider a peripheral device that to many represents the fundamental reason to own a microcomputer. As you may know, there are centrally located large computers that can be accessed by the use of what are called *computer terminals.* A terminal looks like a microcomputer but in fact has no computational capability. It is merely an input keyboard and an output CRT or printer. Its value derives from the fact that it can be connected to a distant central computer, usually by a telephone that is used to call the computer, and is then plugged into the terminal. The terminal sends its input from the keyboard to the central computer over the telephone line and gets back output to its screen or printer the same way. The company that owns or operates the central computer charges the user a small fee to maintain and use files and to use the programs of the big machine. Often, these programs and files are unavailable elsewhere. For example, stock market data can be called up from the main computer, and these data may include not only today's prices, but files of quotations over periods of several months.

So why not just buy a terminal and be able to access the files and computing power of a large mainframe computer? The answer is fairly simple. Terminals are designed for professional and commercial use. They are made for continuous and heavy keyboard operation and have video monitors of very high resolution that permit extremely sharp images to be formed. For these reasons the cost of a video terminal to connect to a central computer service company is often higher than the price of a microcomputer. And that microcomputer can perform local tasks as well as serve to connect you to a

61

mainframe. But how do you connect your microcomputer to the central system?

By adding a simple peripheral device called a *modem* to a microcomputer and then running a program called a *terminal emulator* that makes the computer simulate, or mimic, a terminal, you can use your telephone to connect your microcomputer to a big mainframe computer. The modem, shown in Figure 25, is a small box that plugs into an output port in your computer. It is then connected to the telephone line in one of two ways. The neatest and most reliable is by plugging the so-called *direct-connect modem* into a modular phone outlet. The *acoustic-coupler modem* has a pair of rubber cuffs at each end of the box. After you have called up the computer, you stuff the handset into the cuffs, and the machines "talk" to each other by beeps and buzzes.

Such services as the CompuServe Corporation provides, in addition to their commercial and business utility information, are specially designed features that may be of practical as well as recreational value for microcomputer owners. The modem, whose name is a contraction *of modulate-demodulate,* which is what the device does to the computer output and input to send and receive them over the telephone line, may be the one peripheral that eliminates the need for others. As long as you subscribe to a network service, the service can provide mass storage and printed output of your own records and materials. You can therefore use the service to store your programs and data, and to print out any reports or other material you want to have as hard copy.

Figure 25: An acoustic coupler MODEM that lets your computer talk to the world. (Photo courtesy of Commodore Business Machines Inc.)

These features provided by a network vary, but in general they can make your microcomputer the equivalent of a terminal on a large machine.

To summarize this heavy technical material we may look at Figure 26. This sketch shows the principal parts of the microcomputer and its peripherals, along with their names and the concepts that each of them represents.

Figure 11 in Chapter 2 is a photograph of a general-purpose home microcomputer

Figure 26: We can see in this diagram that the mass-storage system is both an input and an output device.

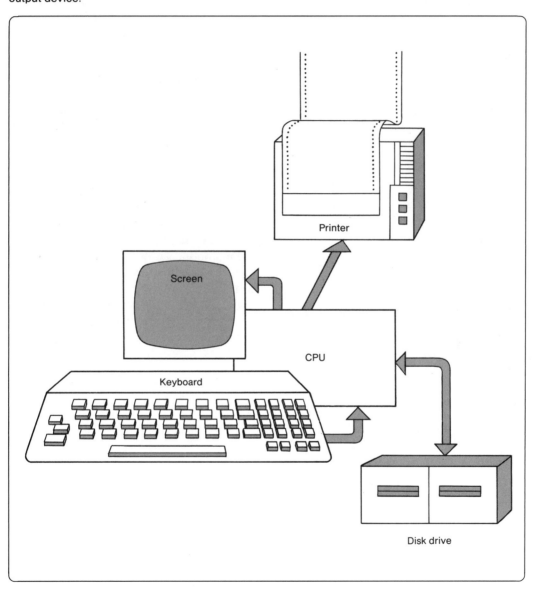

system, consisting of the computer, its associated video monitor and a dot matrix printer for output, a keyboard for input, a dual-floppy disk mass storage system, and a cassette recorder as a secondary mass storage backup. Such a system represents a highly advanced microcomputer capability that could easily serve an educational, commercial, or entertainment role in your home. It could easily provide the following functions:

1. Teaching new skills via programmed instruction
2. Games and recreational computing
3. Word processing
4. General ledger
5. Inventory
6. Accounts payable and receivable
7. Information management
8. Mailing list and label making
9. Business and economic forecasting
10. Graphics
11. Statistical analysis
12. Data communications
13. Electronic mail
14. Information access via commercial networks

And what might a system needed to do these jobs cost? First, you need a computer, which may cost as little as $500; then a video monitor for primary output, about $200; a mass storage system consisting of both a cassette deck (for backup) and a single disk drive, costing about $500; and finally an inexpensive printer costing perhaps $600. The total comes to less than $2000. If you cut out the printer and use your own TV, the price drops to about $1000. And with the appropriate programs or software, which should be acquired slowly, all the jobs listed here can be accommodated. The software costs may range from less than ten dollars for some game programs and educational material, to several hundred dollars for professionally useful business and commercial bookkeeping software. If you want to contact a central service such as CompuServe, add a modem for between $100 and $300, and your software needs decline sharply. But before you rush out to get all this stuff, let us back into the question of how these machines do the things we have been talking about. How do they teach arithmetic and spelling? How can they maintain your business records? We have hinted at the answer when we mentioned programs. We must now address the issue of what programs are.

Chapter 5
Programming by, for, and with Children

Now the chips are down. We have toured the microcomputer from keyboard to ROM, from CRT to floppy disks, from daisy wheels to Winchesters. It is time to roll up our sleeves. In some ways this is the best time of all. If you and your child have never before actually written a program to make a computer do its thing, you are in for an intellectual thrill. Some children at age 6 are ready to try their hand at programming. We generally accept kids starting from age 8 for our regular programming classes. The only specific skill a child needs before starting to write programs is letter-number familiarity. If the child can recognize the letters and numbers on the screen and on the keyboard, the time is right. There is really nothing like the experience of finding out how to do something that was rumored to be arcane and ends up comprehensible.

When you write a computer program, you must often change certain well-established habits. For example, I have always been a person who expects to understand a problem and quickly see a way to solve it. If I cannot get an answer on my own, I turn for help to someone else. This way of coping has generally stood me in good stead; that is, I usually get most of my problems solved. The problem posed by the need or desire to write a computer program will not fall to this method. You often do not see in general how the problem will be solved. That is because the solution is never a general one. A computer program is always specific and intrinsically relevant to the problem to be solved. You must gnaw at the problem one step at a time. Often you do not see where you are going until you almost pass the finish.

The fact is that my old way to solve problems is one I learned as a child. I was told that I must learn to "understand." That meant I must learn global generalities that would help me to solve many kinds of problems. Well, it will not work for computer programming. I found this out most forcefully when one of the adults in our school (remember, we teach adults too!) threatened to quit because he did not understand what he was doing. "What do you mean?" I asked. "Well," he said, "I get the program written alright, but if I try to make it clearer and understandable, it stops working." He had discovered that our classic notion of clarity and understanding often meant vagueness, and worse, logical inconsistency. What computer programming requires is literal adherence to simple logical forms. Problems must be broken down into their most trivial and detailed elements. Only then can we make these machines, which have no claim to understanding or clarity, comprehend clearly what they are to do.

The consequence of this need for precision and clarity is that children have little difficulty getting the point. They are aware that certain ways of acting and talking do not get the job done. They cannot always find the correct path to the goal, but they do recognize an appropriate response when shown one. The result is that children do quite well at programming if someone is there to help them get out of snarled logic. That is why we always have two teachers in our school; the second one looks for problems as they develop and moves to solve them on a one-on-one basis.

First of all, what is a program? It is nothing more nor less than a set of explicit instructions that require the computer to do something. Let us observe initially that we can instruct the computer to do some things even without programming it. For example, we can turn it on and off if we can find the power switch and it is plugged into a wall outlet. Do not sell this point too short! It is often hard to find the power switch on a computer. The reason is that if the switch is too obvious or too obtrusive it might be turned off by accident. Remember what happens to the information in RAM if the power goes. Good-bye memory!

On some machines the power switch can be turned on and off only with a key. The point to remember is that on many microcomputers the power switch does more than simply apply an electric current to the machine. Often, the initial application of power will cause the computer to run a little program of its own to check for faulty chips or other defects. These diagnostic programs are stored in ROM, of course, so they are always there

in dormant form even without power. But the point of these remarks is to try to expose the essential nature of *instructions* as that term applies to mechanical devices. Although we think of information and instruction as properties or qualities of intellectual activity, these concepts are in fact quite relevant to nonintelligent devices like computers or refrigerators.

As we saw previously, the instructions that the CPU can execute are all based on a mathematical-logical-electrical language, although one does not need to understand that language to program a microcomputer. This language is the language of 0 and 1, ON and OFF, opened and closed, and binary numbers, which Claude Shannon of the Bell Telephone Laboratories called bits, from BInary digiTS. The large-scale integrated circuits (LSI) of the CPU (central processing unit) and the RAM and ROM memories of a microcomputer are made up mostly of tiny switches. Because the state of a switch is either open or closed, ON or OFF, set or reset, the states of the LSI chip can be represented by a sequence of bits; 0 for OFF, 1 for ON. If a string of such numbers is cleverly translated into a stream of electrical impulses, the switches inside the chip can be set and reset to represent electrically a path through the chip that is unique for every binary number combination. Since the switches in the central processor are organized into 8-bit units called bytes (remember?), each byte represents one of 256 different symbols. That is because there are 256 ways to arrange eight binary digits (Table 2).

The architecture of the CPU is arranged so that the address bus can accommodate two bytes at a time. The result is that the CPU can be made to request information from one of 65,536 memory locations

Table 2

In this table we use 0 to represent the OFF position and 1 to mean ON.

1. 00000000	•	129. 10000000	•
2. 00000001	•	130. 10000001	•
3. 00000010	•	131. 10000010	•
4. 00000011	•	132. 10000011	•
5. 00000100	•	133. 10000100	•
6. 00000101	•	134. 10000101	•
•	•	•	•
•	•	•	•
•	•	•	•
•	•	•	•
•	•	•	•
•	•	•	•
•	•	•	•
•	•	•	•
•	•	•	•
•	•	•	•
•	•	•	•
•	•	•	•
•	•	•	•
•	•	•	•
•	123. 01111010	•	251. 11111010
•	124. 01111011	•	252. 11111011
•	125. 01111100	•	253. 11111100
•	126. 01111101	•	254. 11111101
•	127. 01111110	•	255. 11111110
•	128. 01111111	•	256. 11111111

each time two strings of 8 bits (or 2 bytes in computer language) are sent over the bus to the memory. This is because two raised to the sixteenth power, or 256 times 256, equals 65,536.

So, in principle, if you carefully prepared a list of binary numbers that directed the CPU to execute one or another of its possible actions, such as comparing two strings of bits and setting another switch to 1 if the two were equal and to 0 if not, you would have written a machine-language program that would let the computer compute the equality of two quantities. Such tasks were the original province of computer programmers. They worked down at the machine-language level, fashioning what were essentially trivial solutions to complicated problems.

The needs of the computer users forced an historical trend away from this method of programming. Often a user had a problem he could not clearly explain to the programmer. The result was chaos. The user needed to write the program. But the requisite experience the program-writing task required is long and arduous. This is because the program language involves complex logical concepts to be expressed in a numerical code that is itself unfamiliar. The result of these constraints on the practical use of computers was the invention of high-level programming languages. These programming languages made it possible to instruct the computer in an approximation of human language. Now the high-level languages have been so refined that programming is quite obviously child's play, and many children do it.

When microcomputers came along, many programs already existed to solve a variety of difficult problems that were the bread and butter of the big machines. The problems they handled in the early days were mostly large-scale mathematical calculations, such as actuarial tables for insurance companies or trajectories of cannon shells or missiles. These big machines were also programmed to do various nonmathematical business tasks, such as printing out 10,000 payroll checks each week with appropriate deductions for taxes, dependents, insurance, and so on. But such programs did little for the person with the personal computer. This fact gave birth to a new cottage industry in the United States: writing programs for little computers.

Once the programming languages were available to smooth the way, anyone who could write a program to balance a checkbook did so. These and other household programs often left a great deal to be desired. They were frequently incomplete, either in the program itself or in the instruction manuals that were included with the programs. Sometimes they generated actual errors in their calculations. It was and still is clear that unless you can "clean up" the details of some of these programs by rewriting sections yourself, they are best left on the store shelf.

For example, consider a program that purports to teach your child the multiplication tables. In most computer languages, the symbol for multiplication is the asterisk (*). This symbol is used to keep the computer from being confused about whether it is supposed to multiply two numbers together or print the letter X. I have a program that uses the little star as the symbol for multiplying even at the level of the problems presented to a child. This is simply a foolish mistake on the part of the programmer. It can easily be corrected, even by someone who cannot write the program, if they know how and where to look for the symbol and how to change it into the familiar ×.

We must now turn to a large question that will separate the men from the boys and the women from the girls. If, as the last few sentences suggest, there is a whole industry aimed at supplying programs (or software) for microcomputers, why would anyone want to "roll their own"? The answer is threefold: (1) You may not find what you want, (2) good programs cost quite a bit, and (3) it's fun to do it yourself. It is also true that although we may be too old to worry about what we do not know, our children are not. Our children need to know about computer programming. Since they do, then maybe we need to know something about it too. We may not be able to solve their problems, but we ought to know how to listen.

Most commercially prepared programs are designed for a mass market. That is to say, in order to sell enough copies the program has to serve the needs of many people. At the family level, however, our needs for computer programs are usually idiosyncratic. What we want are programs that may be highly specific to our own family. A story told to me recently shows how specific some programs have to be. A father programmed his home computer so that his son couldn't play computer games until he had finished his homework —on the computer. One afternoon the father came in and found his son playing a game on the machine much earlier than the boy usually got to the games. He asked his son if the homework was finished. "How could it not be?" was the glib answer, given with a downturned eye. Later the father found that his son had written his own program that bypassed the homework and went directly to the Asteroid Invasion.

The fun of computer programming was touched on when we talked earlier about the general benefits of developing the skill.

Programming by, for, and with Children

The joys of success in mental effort are well known. The facts of program writing lead me to believe that at many steps in the task of writing a program there are mini-triumphs that are quite personal. You can hardly tell someone that you have figured out a new way to fire a space cannon. But the new parts of the computer code that now make the cannon shell explode into a thousand fragments when it hits the target can be truly splendid. Even a little change in a prompting message that clears up some ambiguity in a store-bought program can be fun to do. It makes the program a personal possession that contains part of your own thinking. So let us get into this programming game and see what the issues are. You may find that as an exercise of will and patience it is not your cup of tea. But then again you may love it.

First we must agree to use some popular programming language. As we have mentioned, BASIC is the most common and widely used language. Indeed, every microcomputer that can be purchased on the open market today is either set up to use BASIC from a machine-language program in its ROM, or it can have an equivalent machine-language program loaded into its RAM from a mass storage system. The first arrangement depends on what is called a BASIC interpreter in firmware; the second loads a BASIC interpreter from software. Consequently, because of its absolute availability and universality, we will use BASIC as our prime example of a high-level programming language that you and your child can use to write programs. There are, of course, other programming languages, and we will discuss some of them later.

The BASIC language was invented by John Kemeny and Thomas E. Kurtz as a programming language that would be easy to use for first-time programmers. Many of the features of BASIC, such as its use of English words for commands, are aimed to simplify the amount of material that has to be remembered. But even though it is simple in form and content, it is a language with enormous programming power. Although other special languages are useful for special purposes, like COBOL, which is designed for business applications, BASIC is a general-purpose language. It may not be as efficient as the FORTRAN language for a scientific problem, but it can solve the problem. BASIC is a loose and un-structured language, unlike Pascal, which makes you think first and program later. But this freedom to roam around in the program provides a friendliness to the code, which although infuriating at times,

does not force you to plan every step before you begin. This, to me, means that BASIC offers the opportunity for creativity at every stage in program writing. You may not generate the perfect program the first time out, but it will work—more or less— and that is what counts.

Before we enter this BASIC world of programming, there are one or two things you should know. Although the American Standards Institute will shortly establish an American standard BASIC, probably by early 1983, every manufacturer of small computers has implemented this pro-gramming language in special ways to provide unique (they hope) advantages. Most of these BASIC "dialects" are quite similar. However, to ensure compatibility with different computers I will occasionally indicate that some command or other is

Figure 27: A flashing cursor is shown in the lower right corner of this screen, waiting for your input. (Photo courtesy of Radio Shack, a division of Tandy Corporation)

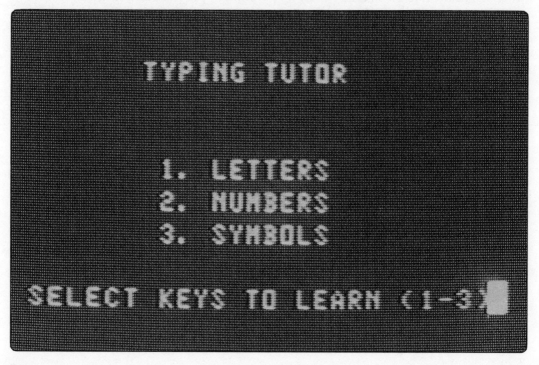

or is not available on some particular machine. For example, the Hewlett-Packard HP-85 uses the direct command SCRATCH to erase a program in computer memory, whereas the Commodore PET® uses the direct command NEW for the same purpose.

Another technical detail which may vary from machine to machine must be reviewed: the cursor. If a microcomputer uses some form of video screen for display of information, as almost all of them do, there will be a symbol that appears on this screen that shows where a keystroke to the keyboard will display a letter on the screen. This cursor symbol—sometimes a flashing square or a flashing or stationary underline mark—can usually be moved around on the screen by keys (cursor control keys) that permit you to revise or correct the screen text. If your machine does not permit such *screen editing,* there will be other procedures that can be used to change information on the screen. On some machines this requires that you change from programming mode to editing mode and then use special symbols to change the program. These symbols are usually letters, which in this special mode do not print as letters but serve as commands to alter parts of the program. We will assume your machine permits cursor editing and will refer to cursor locations to help you orient to where on the screen certain displays will appear.

There are two final points you must keep in mind. All computers distinguish between the letter *l* and the number 1. Children find this distinction clear and obvious, but some touch typists consistently *crash* their programs because of this confusion. Last but not least, the capital letter *O* and the number 0 must also be consistently distinguished. As we shall see, computers force us to make a very

strong distinction between letters and numbers that are used to calculate. This means that an address could have a zero represented by a capital *O* without harm, but if the *O* is used for a zero in a checkbook program it will fail to operate.

The flow of a program proceeds through time, and short though the times are, some things come before others. A computer executes its instructions one at a time (in rare cases a few at a time). This order of execution of program commands is a central feature of all programming languages. In BASIC the order of program steps is generated and preserved by numbering the instructions in the order that they are to be executed. These instruction numbers are called *program line numbers* or just line numbers. Computers that use BASIC as their programming language only accept whole numbers as line numbers, like 10, 260, 38, but not decimals or fractions like 26.352. One might reasonably expect then to start a program at line number 1 and go to 2, 3, 4, and so on. But the designers of BASIC knew that people are not perfect. Often, an unanticipated instruction is needed between, say, 3 and 4. Don't worry. Because the computer only sees the order of the numbers, most programmers use numbers in steps of, say, 10. This means that the first instruction may be numbered 10, the second 20, and so on. If a new instruction is needed between the first and second command, we can therefore use 15 or 13 or 19. Not only can you add new instructions between old ones, but because the computer keeps track of the instruction numbers, you can even add instruction number 16 after you have entered number 20. When the program is executed by the computer, the order will be straightened out automatically.

As you work at the computer keyboard entering your line-numbered instructions, you will be able to see what you are doing because the output screen echoes your keystrokes. That means that when you type the number 30, the number appears on the screen. The appearance of the number on the screen should not lead you to believe that the CPU has recorded the number or that the number has been stored anywhere in the computer's memory. Indeed, during the entry of either program instructions or data, the screen is serving merely as a scratch pad. The CPU only *reads* the instruction after the single most important key on the keyboard has been pressed. This is the ENTER or RETURN or END LINE key. Nothing on the screen has any meaning for the computer until the RETURN key is pressed. Figure 28 shows where the ENTER or RETURN key is located on most keyboards.

You will recall that the parts of the computer are arranged as shown in the diagram in Chapter 2, Figure 3. There is an input, an output, the processor, and the memory that you, the operator, can use and change. All the other stuff is secondary and peripheral. In general terms every computer program is designed to accept some kind of input, process it, and display or print some kind of output. It may also store some of the information for later use. The main point is for you to get the nature of the flow clear: input . . . processing . . . output. As a result of this general program form, there must be instructions for the computer that enable it to accept and retain information entered by the operator and other instructions to format and display output. In the BASIC language these two functions are performed

Figure 28: The RETURN key is usually on the right side of the keyboard in the middle row. (Photo courtesy of Franklin Computer Corporation)

by the commands INPUT and PRINT. When the programmer requires the computer to accept information from the user, the INPUT command is used. If data or other information are to be displayed or printed, the programmer uses the PRINT command.

With these two general ideas, (1) numbering the instructions to control the order of execution of commands and (2) directing the machine to accept input and display output to the outside world, we are ready to write our first program. The program that we write will demonstrate two major properties of microcomputers that make them valuable aids. First, they can accept and operate on "English" words and not just on numbers like a calculator. Second, they are able to store generalized instructions for use with any arbitrary letters or numbers. We will not yet see the most important features of a computer: its ability to store extremely large quantities of information and the speed with which this information can be processed. These properties of the computer will emerge in all their glory later as our programming skills increase.

Somewhere on the keyboard there may be a key or a pair of keys to be pressed successively that will move the cursor to the upper left corner of the screen or that will print a prompting symbol, often the mark > , at the top left corner of the screen. Find that key and press it so that the cursor, or prompt, is at the top of the screen at the first *screen column*. Now press the key that represents the number 1. This may be the top left key, or it may be a key on a special numeric keypad to the right of the main keyboard. Now type in the number 0. These numbers signify to the machine that instruction number 10 is about to be entered. Carefully type the letters INPUT NAME$ next to the number

10, not forgetting to type the dollar sign after the E. We will return shortly to the meaning of the cryptic $. After typing in this command, press RETURN, or whatever the end-of-line key on your machine may be called. This key is probably located on the right side of the main keyboard at the right end of the second or third row. Now the cursor will fly back to the left margin to the second *screen line*. Type in 20 PRINT "HELLO "; NAME$ and press RETURN. Notice as you enter command 20 that a space is to be left after the 0 of HELLO, and that a ; separates the quoted word from the unquoted NAME$. The space inside the quotes after HELLO serves to leave a space after the computer prints the symbols H E L L O. Computers do not know where words start and end, and when they store information, they strip away blanks unless those spaces are inside quotation marks. Now type in 30 END, and the program is complete. The screen of your computer should look like this:

```
10 INPUT NAME$
20 PRINT "HELLO    ";NAME$
30 END
```

On some machines, the Apple for example, you may need a special command to tell the machine that you are not drawing pictures, but rather are using words. For these machines you may need a line, say 5, followed by the command TEXT.

Let us first analyze what this program will do and then consider how it works. The typing in of this *code* has resulted in a program residing in the RAM memory of the computer. How can we prove this? Find a way to clear the screen of its current information. This is usually done by a keyboard key marked CLEAR, CLR, CLEAR SCREEN, or some such.

Some machines require that you type in the word HOME and press RETURN. Once the screen is clear you may think, Well, good-bye program. But that is not the case. We will now enter a command that does not need a line number; it is called a *direct command* and is entered by typing the word LIST, followed by a tap on the RETURN key. Wow, look at the program zip back! You know the program was in memory, for you see that when you type LIST and then press RETURN, it reappears on the screen. This program will continue to reside in the computer's memory until either the machine is turned off, or new commands are entered using the same line numbers. We could if we wished type in a direct command that would clear the computer's memory the way the keyboard CLEAR key clears the screen. That command is NEW, or in some BASIC dialects, SCRATCH.

Once you are convinced that the program is still there, we can make the computer execute the program by typing the direct command RUN. This command instructs the computer to search for the lowest numbered instruction, execute it, fetch the next lowest numbered instruction, execute it, and so on. When it comes to an instruction that commands END, the computer is to stop searching for instructions and to return control to the user. Usually when this happens the computer signals termination of the program by printing the word READY or OK or a flashing cursor or both on the screen. If you have typed the RUN command, the first thing that happened is that a question mark was printed on the screen under the word, RUN, and the cursor moved next to the question mark and blinked. This display is the computer's response to the command INPUT. It is a complicated response and requires now that we settle

down and come to grips with the central and most difficult idea in the computer business: the concept of a *variable*.

You will recall that information as well as program instructions are stored in memory boxes called RAM. Any information that the computer needs, whether it is program commands, or information generated by the user at the keyboard, must find a home in RAM memory. This is done at the command RUN. When that direct command is entered, the computer erases all the RAM memory except the program commands. The RAM memory boxes from the bottom of the program to the end of the memory are reserved for use by the internal program requirements of the computer and the information entered by the user. Whenever the program requests information from the user, a starting memory box is reserved under the variable name. In this example that name would be NAME$. Some machines will not permit such long names for variables. You may have to use a single letter like N$.

Variable names that end with a dollar sign designate memory locations that simply store keystrokes, whether they are letter or number keys. They are called *string variables*. If numbers are stored in memory under $ variables, those numbers are only symbols: that is, they have no numeric properties. Two of them cannot be added together. They act like address numbers or the numbers on the backs of football players. If a variable name like NA is used to reserve a memory location, that location reserves space for a number that is really a number. Variable names without the dollar sign are *numeric variables*.

After the name is entered on the screen *scratch pad* and the RETURN key pressed, the computer counts the number of letters that were typed to the screen and allocates enough memory starting at the first box to store the input string of symbols. The machine also makes a mark (called a *pointer*) at the last box that was used so it is ready to store the next block of information starting at the next unused memory box.

When the program ran, the input command printed a question mark on the screen as a prompt that keyboard input was expected. Whatever was typed to the screen after the prompt would be memorized (in the arbitrarily assigned memory boxes) as soon as the RETURN key was pressed. Furthermore, those symbols that the user typed into this program would be stored in a memory location named NAME$. So after executing command 10, the computer had established a starting memory location named NAME$, printed a question mark on the screen, and waited for keystroke inputs followed by the RETURN key. When the RETURN key was pressed, presumably after a name was typed on the keyboard, those letters were captured and stored under the name NAME$. The symbol $ after the name indicates to the computer to recognize the input keystrokes merely as symbols or letters, not as numbers. It identifies the variable name as a *string* variable.

At this point the computer jumps to the next instruction line and executes command 20. This command directs the computer to output to some device, usually the CRT, any symbols that follow the PRINT command. If the symbols are enclosed in double quotes, they are to be printed literally to the output device. If the symbol names a memory location, as NAME$ does, the contents of that memory location are to be copied and printed. Stress to yourself the point that the computer merely copies the contents of memory NAME$ and does not destroy the memory.

Because the contents of NAME$ were input by the user, the program displays on the output device information that was not preplanned or prerecorded. Rather the computer used information inserted by the user to generate output that is unique to the user. We might expect this sequence to appear on the screen if we ran our program:

RUN
> (This is the command we type to get the program going.)

?   John Brown [RETURN]
> (This is the input prompt [?], followed by our typing a name and a press of the RETURN key.)

HELLO John Brown
> (This is the computer's PRINT message.)

READY
> (This shows that the program has completed its run.)

Kids and Computers

We could improve the quality of the program by replacing the mysterious question mark with a new command that printed TYPE YOUR NAME on the screen first. Because we want this "instruction to the user" to appear first, we will have to command the computer to print its message before it asks for input. We can do this by using line number 5 to make the program look like the one to the right: ⇨

```
 5  PRINT "TYPE YOUR NAME"
10  INPUT NAME$
20  PRINT "HELLO ";NAME$
30  END
```

Now the advantage of starting at line 10 and going in steps of 10 in the line numbering becomes clear. If we had started the program at line 1, we would have had no room to insert this additional command without renumbering the whole program. Although some microcomputers can do this renumbering act by a single direct command, most of them require that we go through the program and tediously retype each line number.

These four numbered lines of program instruction would lead to the display given at the right when the screen was cleared and RUN was entered: ⇨

```
RUN
TYPE YOUR NAME
? Jane Green
HELLO Jane Green
READY
```

A point we should note is the use of the semicolon as a separator or delimiter between the literal information to be printed and the contents of the memory box that is also printed out. Some computers do not require this delimiter to connect parts of the same line; others use other symbols. The point is that if more than a single unit of information is to be put together on a single line, some kind of delimiter is needed simply to restrain the computer from making a carriage return to the next line and printing something like: ⇨

```
HELLO
Jane Green
```

76

The final program command we will describe in this chapter is termed LET. This command is used inside a program to fill a particular memory location with some data, either string information or numbers. The command is used in the right-hand column to enter symbols into memory from inside a program: ⇨

```
1 LET I$ = "TYPE YOUR NAME"
```

The equal sign is used to denote "be," not "equal to." If such a line were inserted in our sample program, we could then revise line 5 to read: ⇨

```
1 LET I$ = "TYPE YOUR NAME"
5 PRINT I$
10 INPUT NAME$
20 PRINT "HELLO ";NAME$
30 END
```

If we added a new line 2, ⇨

```
1 LET I$ = "TYPE YOUR NAME"
2 LET H$ = "HELLO "
5 PRINT I$
10 INPUT NAME$
20 PRINT H$;NAME$
30 END
```

we would then have replaced all the print command literal strings of symbols with equivalent variable names whose memory locations contained those symbol strings. Once again notice that if we want to separate the word HELLO from the name, we must include the space as part of the symbol string that is stored in H$.

The LET command is obviously related to the INPUT command. Indeed it does from inside the program what the INPUT command does from the keyboard. Notice that for the programs we have written the LET command is unnecessary. Later we shall see that this command will let us revise stored information from inside the program without having to get new information from the keyboard.

Kids and Computers

Before we continue with some new concepts, we need to review and get clear the idea of naming memory locations in which information like names or numbers that are typed into the computer are stored. In our previous example, we used the symbol NAME$ to name the memory locations that would store our input information. We could just as well have used the symbol X$, or the symbol G3$. Most microcomputers permit us to use single letters, a letter and a number, or double letters to name a memory location. Why then could we get away with NAME$ if only single or double symbols are allowed? Many computers permit us to add irrelevant letters to a variable name so that the name will be easier to remember. The computer in our example actually stored the typed-in name in a memory location named NA$, which is the shortened version of NAME$. We could just as easily have written line 20 as   ⇨

```
20  PRINT H$;NA$
```

You will recall that these names of memory locations are technically called *variables*. This is because, as you may have noticed in our example, the name entered in the first run, John Brown, and in the second run, Jane Green, both went to the same location. This means that although the name (and consequently the location of the memory box) remains fixed, the contents can vary from one run of the program to another. This is one of the really powerful ideas contained in computers. Once a memory location has been reserved by giving it a name like NA$, its contents can be replaced any time the program is rerun. Even when the program is not run again, if the program uses the same name later for a second INPUT, the new material that is entered will overwrite the existing information.

78

Suppose when the computer asked for input by displaying the ? input prompt, you did not enter any keystrokes, but just pressed the RETURN key. The result is that you might bounce out of the program, and the computer would print READY, just as it would if it reached END. This means that the computer is no longer running the program. In order for the program to run, you would have to retype the direct command RUN. As we shall see later, you could also use another direct command to restart the program, the CONT (for CONTinue) command.

We saw that we can use a variable name like NAME$, which is four letters long, while the computer only reads the first two. This points up the fact that the computer often disregards irrelevant information that is entered into it. For example, line 10 of our preceding program looked like: ⇨

> 10 INPUT NAME$

It might just as well have been written, ⇨

> 10INPUTNA$

Microcomputers often disregard spaces and extra letters in program instructions. We take advantage of this feature (if your computer permits it) to make our program lines more readable. One more point on variable names: If you tried to use OR as a variable name, the computer would reject it and report a SYNTAX ERROR. This is because these letters are a word reserved by the computer for its instruction code. Most computers reserve about 90 letter pairs that cannot be used for variable names.

Let us pause now to summarize our current knowledge about programming microcomputers. We have seen that microcomputers operate using machine language down at the level of the CPU. Scientists and engineers have advanced the programming art by inventing high-level programming languages like BASIC. These languages use English words to form the set of commands that the computer follows. A program for the computer is a sequence of commands, written in numbered lines, executed in the order they are numbered. Some commands can be issued to the machine outside a program. These are the *direct* commands: LIST, to show the current program in memory; NEW or SCRATCH, to clear the memory of the current program; and RUN, to make the computer execute the program that currently resides in RAM.

The commands we have used so far that appear inside the programs are as follows: PRINT, to get information out of the computer onto the screen or printer; INPUT, to request information from the user to be stored in memory locations identified by variable names; LET, to assign some symbols or a number to a variable name; and END, to terminate program control of the machine. Variable names define two distinct kinds of memory locations. String variables can be recognized because they end with a dollar sign ($) in every BASIC dialect. These are the variables that accept any symbol as their input information. Numeric variables need have no distinctive mark. They designate memory locations that only accept numbers that can be manipulated arithmetically.

Finally, we should recall that the logic of a computer program consists in commanding the computer to perform simple functions in a specific order. These functions involve the input of information, storage of the information in appropriate formats, operations performed on the information (all this to be discussed later), and printing out or outputting the information. Figure 29 shows what some would call a *block diagram,* that connects this logical flow to the specific steps described here.

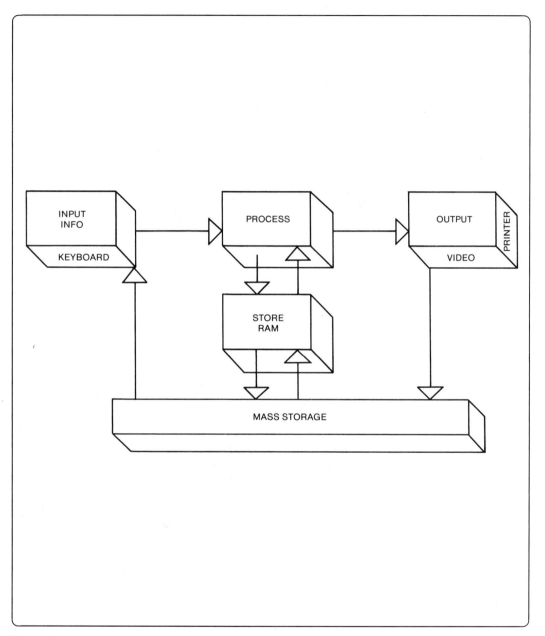

Figure 29: A block diagram of the information flow in a microcomputer. Notice again that mass storage may serve for input, output, and memory.

Kids and Computers

Now we try COMPUQUIZ #2. This one is both easier and harder than the first, but try it; you will find it of value to refresh your memory of this difficult material.

COMPUQUIZ #2

1. What does the NEW or SCRATCH command do to the program in memory?

2. What happens when you enter the command LIST and, of course, (you forgot, didn't you) press the RETURN key?

3. LET is a command that does two things: It fills a variable with information, and it also performs certain numerical operations. What would the variable X contain after the line LET X = 5 + 3 was executed?

4. What symbol must occur at the end of any variable symbol that holds only string information and not numerical information?

5. Could the symbol in question 3 have been X$? If not, why?

6. What does the direct command RUN do?

7. How does the computer know that it has come to the end of the program and should stop running?

We will leave computer programming now to examine ways to use a computer that depend on the handiwork of others. As we learn about using these "canned" programs, we should note that the logic of these programs conforms to the general principles shown here. After that short excursion into the software marketplace, we will return to the programming problems with a new conviction that, as an old English schoolmaster once said about mathematics, "What one fool can do, another can also."

Chapter 6

Running the Machine

If computers are as easy to program as they seem from the last chapter, why would anyone buy programs that were professionally prepared? It is a good question and one that is raised almost daily in business and industry. The effort of learning to program offers rich rewards, but some programming jobs may be too complicated and time consuming to do yourself. For example, in the world of microcomputers game programs are very complicated. Many popular games require perhaps six months or more of programming effort to produce. It is next to impossible to expect an amateur programmer to develop a complicated game without several years of experience.

Large suites of interconnected programs that are useful in business may require professional writers to work for many hundreds and often thousands of hours. That is why businesses are willing to pay from $50,000 to $500,000 for useful programs.

In the microcomputer realm, program size is limited to the size of the memory that is not used by the operating system and is therefore addressable by the CPU. Currently that size is between 30,000 and 45,000 symbols. Since each program line may contain on the average 50 symbols, a large program for a microcomputer might be of the order of 600 lines long. So programs are smaller and more limited in scope. This means they are less costly to develop, and these costs may be spread over larger numbers of purchasers. Keep in mind, however, that newer computers will use CPUs that to all intents and purposes have unlimited addressable memory. The limitations on the new generation of microcomputers may no longer be memory capacity but rather processing speed. The bigger the program the longer it takes to function.

Now let us reverse the question. If fairly inexpensive software is available to endow your microcomputer with sophisticated functional capabilities, why should you do any programming yourself? The fact is that a professionally prepared program to solve a particular problem may not satisfy your tastes or needs, whether the program entertains you and your child, provides practice in arithmetic, maintains your recipes and menus for dinner, or keeps track of your deductibles for the Form 1040. You then have two alternatives. Modify the professionally prepared program or write your own. Again, industry has led the way. Any large computer installation requires a person or a team of programmers to adjust, modify, and enhance professionally prepared material.

Kids and Computers

An example of useful software modification solved the problem of a parent of a child in our school who had purchased an educational program to drill children in arithmetic skills. The father arrived at the school in a panic one day to explain to our dean that his program only did multiplication tables up to 10s. His child's traditionally oriented school required that the multiplication tables be committed to memory up to 12s. Three minutes and two lines of code later the program was set up to ask how large the greatest factor should be. Just to be safe the father input 15 to this prompt, and I suspect that his child is the school multiplying whiz kid.

Often, the need is to connect two independent programs so that they both operate on the same information. For example, you have a list of merchants, companies, doctors, plumbers, etc., that you trade with. You have to pay them, or some group of them, monthly. Those payments from your checkbook may or may not be tax deductible. If you had a program to store your addresses, another to balance your checkbook, and a third to maintain your tax records, it would be convenient to have all three programs connect to each other. Your checkbook would be debited and the name of the creditor recorded at the same time an entry was made about the deductibility of the payment in your tax records.

The software manufacturers are familiar with this problem. Their hope is to design such an integrated package that you need do nothing but load the program into your computer, and it will then do all your jobs. Of course this ideal is rarely met. Even the best programs have a kind of independence from each other. A program that turns your microcomputer into a word processor does such useful work that it is hard to complain if it will not balance your checkbook. A program that lets you see the consequences to budget plans as one or another entry is changed is another example of a useful "stand-alone" program. But it truly would be neat to let the word processor extract information from the economic forecaster in order to help you prepare a report. Perhaps, if you could write programs yourself you could write this "interfacing" program.

Unfortunately, difficulty stands in the way of this plausible suggestion. Many of these professional programs are written, not in the kind of high-level language like BASIC that you would use, but in the computer's machine language. This makes it next to impossible to add the appropriate "hooks" and "inserts" these programs would need to work together. The reason a high-level language is not used is twofold. First, the computer functions faster when programmed in machine language. For programs like word processing, speed is essential since the machine must keep up with you while you type, and move text around at the same time. Second, and often more important to the manufacturers, is the fact that machine-language programs can be more easily protected from unauthorized copying.

The issue of software piracy involves many confusing questions in copyright law. Software is valuable and difficult to protect from theft. Often, people who commit such theft are hardly aware of it. They simply "let their friend copy this new game program they bought." At The Children's Computer School we use commercial programs either purchased for the school or developed by our teachers. This software is used mostly in our Three R's programs for young children. Often, children ask to borrow a program to copy for their use at home. We then have an opportunity to discuss the point of our refusal. Simply put, copying programs is stealing. We do not permit it and neither should you.

Manufacturers of packaged software are beginning to address these various problems. They are moving in two directions. Some, by combining several useful programs into a program suite, are making it easier to access the additional features people want. Others are writing programs in BASIC and in other high-level languages that the user can work with easily. For the manufacturer's protection these programs may be guarded from theft by internal codes. Their *documentation,* the manuals of instruction and procedures for use, may also be sufficiently elaborate and carefully prepared that the cost of duplicating the manual is too high for the pirate.

But regardless of the solutions software manufacturers may devise, nothing can substitute for an acquaintance with programming. This need for such knowledge and understanding was brought home to me personally by experiences at The Children's Computer School. We had no sooner admitted our first class of children when a parent approached the registrar and said, "Why don't you offer a programming course for parents, so we can know what our children are learning?" Within two months the number of adult students in our school exceeded the number of children. Even now, adults and children enroll in our programming courses in about equal numbers.

Some adults come to our school to keep up with their kids. But more and more we see people coming to us because they want to find out about the computer revolution. One of the most popular parts of the adult program is learning the strange names and acronyms that computer lingo is filled with. Such esoterica as RAM, ROM, CPU, CRT, software, floppies, and so on, have so caught the popular imagination that people want to know what these terms mean. Indeed, our introductory program has been so successful that more than 40% of the adults continue past the novice course to intermediate and advanced programming. Many of these students have used the knowledge they acquire from us to help them make business and personal decisions about buying computers. They have learned what to look for and how to avoid overbuying for their own needs. Probably the most important thing they have learned is how to analyze the problems they want to solve in terms that a computer may use. (We will be reviewing just these issues in Chapter 8.)

Even the most knowledgeable programmer buys some programs, because it is often worthwhile to have immediate use of a good program that runs. Furthermore, if the program code is available to you, by *listing* the program you may find hints and kinks that will improve your or your child's own programming. As we shall see in the next chapter, useful *subroutines* can be learned that will make your own programs better. The novice to computing will also find that store-bought programs will provide experience in computer operation, as distinct from computer programming. Often, complex commercial programs require the development of skill in machine use that is helpful in its own right. (For example, a good word processing program may help a youngster learn to type.) This line is often quoted by people who support the value of computer games as a means to develop motor and eye-hand coordination. A child or adult who has mastered "star shooter" has clearly developed a new skill. The real question is whether this skill transfers in some way to other skills or knowledge. We shall not attempt to answer this question now (but see Chapter 9). However, I should point out that skill transfer is fundamental to the generalization of knowledge. Note, however, that not every skill has transfer value.

Store-bought programs come in two main forms. The first kind of program is ROM based in the sense that a new ROM chip (or chips) is added to the existing ROM in the computer. This is usually done by means of a *cartridge* or other device that plugs into a slot or *user port* on the host machine. This is a common way to market programs for game playing with a home computer. The advantage to the manufacturer is that the program is not easily copied, and because these programs are written in machine language they make fast-moving video displays possible. The drawback is that such programs will only work on machines for which they were designed. They lack the central programming quality of *transportability*—the possibility of running the same program on a variety of machines. In principle, BASIC programs written without fancy frills can be used with any machine that can be programmed in BASIC.

The second kind of program is written onto a mass storage medium, usually a cassette tape or a floppy disk. This kind of program can be loaded into the host machine by inserting the medium into the mass storage device and loading, or booting, the program into computer RAM. Sometimes, mass-storage-based programs also require a special ROM chip. In that case the ROM chip or a circuit board containing the chip(s) must be installed inside the machine by a technician. The ROM remains dormant in the machine until the program calls on it for specialized functions. Such programs are usually complex and

serve a single useful function, such as word processing or data base management.

The availability of programs for purchase is an important feature that computer manufacturers advertise. Therefore, in the selection of a home computer one main criterion is the availability of a large library of programs useful in your home or for your children. We will return to this point when we talk more about selecting your own computer.

Even though the use of programs does not in and of itself require any programming skills, it is necessary that you know how to get them to work. In the case of cartridge-based (whole program in ROM) programs, the instruction sheet is sufficient to operate the system. For mass-storage-based programs you must use some programming code to get the program into your machine and working. Usually the instruction sheet or manual tells how to do this. The general idea is often glossed over, so we will examine what happens in some detail when a program is used with a home computer.

Programs for use on microcomputers are generally bought recorded on a mass storage medium. This medium must be played back or read by a mass storage device connected to your computer. The least expensive, and consequently most popular of these devices, is an audiotape cassette machine. These cassette recorders, like all mass storage systems, have to be able to record and play back information. When used to load programs for the computer, they are only used in their playback mode. (Therefore, if you never touch the RECORD key of the cassette system, you will never accidently erase a program on the tape.)

The cassette recorder connects to your computer either by a cable with a single specialized plug, as in the Commodore VIC or PET®, or by three cables with mini-phone plugs on both ends that connect to the computer and the tape deck. The three plugs carry (1) the data from the computer to the tape, (2) data from the tape to the computer and, (3) control signals from the computer to turn the cassette motor on and off. For loading and using commercial programs, only plugs 2 and 3 need to be connected.

There is a new direct command that you need to learn now. Recall the other direct commands that you already know: LIST, RUN, and NEW (or SCRATCH). LIST makes the computer display and program already stored in RAM. RUN makes the computer execute any program stored in RAM, and NEW or SCRATCH erases any program or data in RAM. If there is no program in RAM, none of these commands has any effect. We need a direct command that makes the computer attend to a mass storage peripheral if it is connected and make it play back any program that is stored on its medium. The BASIC command that does this is LOAD or CLOAD, optionally followed by the program name between quotation marks as, for example   ⇨

> LOAD "checkwriter"

When this command is entered by typing it in and pressing the RETURN key, the computer does several things. First, it automatically issues a NEW command to the RAM. This erases whatever happened to be in memory. Then it stores the word *checkwriter* in a string variable, like L$, and turns on a *comparison* program stored in ROM. It may then prompt the user with a screen command such as PRESS THE PLAY KEY. When this has been done by the operator, the computer then activates the motor of the cassette machine and listens at the input port for code that represents the beginning of a program.

Kids and Computers

When it receives this *status* code it stores the first burst of information in another string variable, say P$. At that point the ROM comparison program checks to see if ⇨

$$P\$ = L\$$$

When that equality is satisfied, that is, when the name of the program on tape is *checkwriter,* the computer starts to read the code on the tape and enter it into RAM. At the end of the program, the tape signal contains an *end status* code which the computer reads and then stops the tape drive motor. Usually the computer signifies that the program has been loaded by printing some message like READY to the screen and/or flashing the cursor.

We can get a sense of what happens throughout this lengthy but quickly executed routine by showing what the screen on your computer might look like during this process. We assume the computer is turned on and that the mass storage cassette machine is correctly connected to the computer. The cassette tape containing the program has been inserted in the player and rewound. The video screen looks like this: ⇨

READY

Now you type ⇨

LOAD "checkwriter"

and press RETURN. The screen may then issue this message: ⇨

PRESS "PLAY"
ON THE TAPE CASSETTE

Some machines assume that after you have entered a LOAD command you will know that you must press the PLAY key on the tape deck. The machine will then start the tape drive and may display various status messages. For example, as the tape moves, you would see these messages on the Commodore PET®: ⇨

SEARCHING FOR checkwriter

FOUND star shooter

FOUND checkwriter

LOADING checkwriter

READY

88

You should notice that this cassette tape contains at least two programs. The first is called *star shooter* and was found and passed over by the computer. When the program labeled *checkwriter* appeared, the computer "recognized" it as the requested program and started to load the program, as indicated by the next line. The last message, the READY message, means that control of the RAM has been returned from the cassette machine to the keyboard. At this point, if you enter the direct command RUN, the computer will execute the program. If you were to command LIST, the computer would display the program that had been loaded from the cassette into RAM. Once the READY message has appeared, you should press the STOP key on the cassette deck. You could also rewind the cassette at this time so that you would be ready to reload the program at a later time.

Now that a program is loaded and RUN has been entered, you are ready to use the capabilities of the computer. You will need to know in outline the nature of a typewriter keyboard and be able to tell the difference between letters and numbers. You also need to know how to use the shift key to make capital letters and for other purposes as well. In the last analysis it is up to the program writer to make sure you can use the program. There are two ways to do this, and in high-quality programs both ways are used. They are both called documentation and exist either in a manual or instruction sheets and/or in the computer program itself. Documentation inside the program itself makes the program self-documenting. Such self-documentation often takes several forms, called *input prompting* and *menu displays*. To get a clear idea of how these two kinds of self-documentation work, let us pursue our checkwriter example a little longer.

After the command RUN has been entered, the screen may display:　⇨

Enter today's date as DD/MM/YY
?

Kids and Computers

This is an input prompt asking you to enter the date. The cryptic DD/MM/YY may not be easily understood. Reference to the user's manual should explain that all dates should be entered into this program in the form of three pairs of two-digit numbers— day first, month next, and year last. For example, the manual would show that February 2nd, 1982, should be entered as 02/02/82, whereas June 26th, 1981, should be 26/06/81.

The computer program coding for this first prompt may have looked like this: ⇨

```
10  PRINT "Enter today's date as
    DD/MM/YY"
20  INPUT DA$
```

What the computer did after the RUN command was entered was to go to line 10, execute the program command PRINT, and print the input prompt. It then jumped to the next line, 20, and waited for you to type in your date. When you completed your typing, the data you entered were stored in the computer RAM under the name DA$. Next the computer might prompt you to turn on your printer and load blank checks into it. Then it could flash a menu display on the screen like this: ⇨

```
PRESS THE NUMBER OF THE
TASK YOU WANT TO DO

(1)  Enter deposits
(2)  Transfer to savings
(3)  Write checks
(4)  Print current statement
(5)  Update files
(6)  Exit the program
```

Such a menu gives you the choice of using any of the options the computer has available in this program to handle your check-writing activities. With such great self-documentation you might think, "Why would I need any more instructions?" The answer is that as you wind down into the program, ambiguous prompts and menus are bound to arise. Without a complete handbook to guide you along all the possible routes you could take through the program, you are bound to get stuck. We call this kind of difficulty with even the best programs the "documentation drearies." Any computer program that aims to do something useful or practical faces

90

these pitfalls. The programmer sought to do the best job possible with the least ambiguity and potential for error, but the operator, or user, never seems to think the way the programmer did. Even in game programs, surely the simplest programs to run from the user's point of view, experience or a good review of the instructions helps to make the game more fun.

Menus can be *nested*. This means that an item on the menu leads to a new menu that contains other options. For example, an arithmetic skill-drill program for children might start up with the menu: ⇨

```
What do you want to do?
  (1) Addition
  (2) Subtraction
  (3) Multiplication
  (4) Division
Select the number of the practice
you want to do (   )
```

Suppose the child presses 3 for multiplication. A new menu now appears on the screen: ⇨

```
You picked multiplication
Do you want to change?
Type Y for yes or N for no
```

This simple yes-no choice lets the child change his mind even after he made a choice. Such programming is good form, especially where a segment of the program runs for a long time after the choice. Let us continue by having the child press Y; then a new "command menu" appears: ⇨

```
Enter the highest factor      (   )
Enter the number of
problems                       (   )
Do you want to have timed tries?
  Enter T for timed S for
  untimed                      (   )
```

After the last entry the problems appear. At the end of the selected number of problems the program could figure the score and display the percent correct or some other information. There is no guarantee that such a program will be interesting or even useful to a child, but good program design will help to ensure that the program will not fail because it cannot be understood.

In addition to good input prompts and menus, useful programs need to be made "idiot proof." This is accomplished by writing more program lines than the program actually needs to work. These extra lines are included in the program to catch input accidents. For example, the check-writer program might scan the input string variable to check that six numbers and two slash marks were entered. It could not check the date itself (although some microcomputers have real clocks in them that run all the time), but it can check for the right symbols. Also, a common programming trick is to include a few additional lines of program code that ask the user to check things like dates again and to press a special key, say Y for yes or N for no, before the string variable is stored.

The program example of the children's arithmetic practice used such a check on whether the child had picked the problems he wanted. Such programming touches make the program what the manufacturers call "user friendly." The problem with such user friendly programs is that after you have used them for awhile, all the additional checking keystrokes get to be an annoyance. Best of all would be a program that starts out giving you lots of prompts but lets you or the computer delete the extras after you have spent some time with the program. These adaptable programs are on the way, and as user skill increases, the speed of computer-user interaction will increase because the computer will cut down on requiring so many checks on progress.

Some programs are too big to fit into the limited memory of a microcomputer. In that case programmers resort to the techniques of divide and conquer. The task of the program is broken down into subtasks. Each of the subtasks is then written as a separate program. For example, check-writer may contain one program that lets you enter deposits and withdrawals, another that prints checks, and a third that keeps track of deductible and nondeductible expenditures. The suite of three programs contains commands that let each program load other programs, depending on what you order on the menu. Such program suites comprise what are called *chained* programs. The different programs in the suite are designed to call up the values of the memory boxes they all may need to reference. Some forms of BASIC do not permit program chaining. In that case it is necessary to load successive programs by hand and to recall from mass storage the needed values of the variables in memory.

The ability of a microcomputer to load, or bootstrap, programs written by others extends enormously its practical value. Even without any programming skills you and your child will find a computer can be a useful and convenient appliance. After all, many users of micro- and larger computers in business and industry have no knowledge of programming; yet they get the plane reservations made and the telephone bills sent out. The same thing is true in areas of computer-aided education. Many children are exposed in school to computers that are used to teach and drill in a variety of subjects. These computers are operated by teachers who often know little or nothing about the nature of the programming in these machines. But insofar as a valuable educational experience is provided, one cannot fault teachers for using computers any more than one would object to a bank using them.

A good ready-made commercial program has a sweet sophistication. But the wherewithal to write your own stuff makes even the programs that you buy more interesting. You will find yourself asking, "How did they do that trick?" And when you find out, the pleasure of comprehension is enormous. But enough of this commercial message; let us get back to the computer.

Chapter 7

Kids Can Write Programs

We have seen in Chapter 5 that writing a program in BASIC is rather simple. However, we surely recognized that the program we wrote was trivial, not to say perhaps simpleminded. All the program did was to request a name, retain in memory the name that was typed from the keyboard, and then print out a stored message followed by a copy of the name from memory. That program demonstrated two important functions of a computer: information input and information output. It also showed how the memory can store information that is either contained in the program: the symbols "HELLO ", stored in the variable H$, or entered through the keyboard—the name that was typed. Both sets of symbols were stored in predefined memory boxes called *variables*. The variable was located somewhere in the RAM, but you did not have to know its whereabouts. All you needed in order to recover a copy of the information was its *variable name*. That is, you were able to access the stored information regardless of its physical location. All you needed to know was its logical identity.

These comments point up an important fact about computer programming. In the old days, the programmer had to know all the details about the computer's functions. Today, the high-level program languages like BASIC take care of the housekeeping and make you deal only with the logic and content of the program. This means that once you understand the intrinsic logic of programming, the technical details of computer functions are unimportant.

Program logic has already been introduced by reference to the three program commands that you have learned— PRINT, LET, and INPUT. These commands along with the sequential order of action that is defined by the line numbers are the fundamental features of a program. You have also been introduced to variables and how they are assigned values, but we will say more about that later. There are only two other program command functions of this kind that are needed to write (almost) any program. Both these new commands are used to get around the limitations of the sequential and unswerving progress imposed by the line numbering. They are *branching* commands, program code that forces the order of execution of operations out of the lockstep of the line numbers.

We introduce them by their names. The first is GO TO, often entered as GOTO without the space between the words, followed by a line number, which sends the program to some line number (forward or backward) that is out of the normal numerical sequence of the program lines. When a program gets to a line number with the GOTO command, the program branches to the line specified, skipping everything between the original line that sent it and this new line, which it then immediately executes. The program resumes at that point and continues to execute the line numbers in order.

Let us see the effect of the GOTO command in a program. Recall our program from Chapter 5: ⇨

```
5   PRINT "TYPE YOUR NAME"
10  INPUT NAME$
20  PRINT "HELLO ";NAME$
30  END
```

Whenever we wanted to see the program work, we had to type RUN as a direct command. This direct command made the computer go to the first line of the program in order to execute the program line by line. Because the last line contained the command END, the program ended. If now we enter a new line 30 as ⇨

```
30 GOTO 5
```

the program will never end. When it reaches line 30, it will transfer program command to line 5 which will cause the computer to print a second TYPE YOUR NAME and again pause for input. When a new name is typed in, the computer will overwrite the old name at memory location NAME$ and then proceed to line 20 to print its salutation. It will then reach line 30, where it will go to line 5 and repeat the whole cycle again. The program can only be stopped by pressing the RETURN key without any input or by pressing the BREAK or RESET key. On some machines you can first press a key labeled CTRL or CONTROL and then press the letter C key to break the loop. Such a *loop,* actually an infinite loop, is one technique that can be used to make the computer do the same kind of thing over and over again without intervention.

94

In order to intervene in such a looping process from within the program, it is necessary to make use of another new program command: IF . . . THEN.

The program command IF . . . THEN is probably the most important and significant logical idea possessed by a computer. This command requires the computer to evaluate the statement after the IF. This evaluation is binary. The statement after the IF is either true or false. If the IF statement is true, the command following THEN is executed. By the use of this command the computer is able to make decisions that depend on the logical truth or falsity of either a state of its memory or the value of a variable. To complete our example, if we add line 25 to our program, we can control the loop by the name we type as input. This bit of program code also demonstrates once again that the computer knows nothing about names or anything else; it simply evaluates symbols.   ⇨

```
 5 PRINT "TYPE YOUR NAME"
10 INPUT NAME$
20 PRINT "HELLO ";NAME$
25 IF NAME$ = "STOP" THEN END
30 GOTO 5
```

When we run this program by issuing the RUN command, we first see the message prompt to type our name. If we enter our name, then at line 20 our name will be printed after the word HELLO. Line 25 must be ignored by the computer, since NAME$ does not equal "STOP." Therefore the computer goes to line 30 which forces it to line 5. At line 5 it again prompts for our name. Suppose now we type in the letters S T O P. At line 20 the computer will print HELLO STOP to the screen and then at line 25, since NAME$ does equal "STOP" the computer executes the THEN command and ceases program execution.

Because it looks silly to have the computer print a foolish display like HELLO STOP, we could prevent this by changing line 25 to line 15. This is easy to do because changing a line number and

then pressing RETURN will restore the line
with the new number. The old line number
25 will still be in the program. To get rid
of it, we merely type 25 followed by a
RETURN. This enters line 25 without any
commands. It makes line 25 a null line,
like every other unused line number.

Let us pause now to review the material
on programming that we have covered
so far. The purpose of this break is to get
you and your child set to write a program
of your own that will make use of some or
all of the program and direct commands
that you have seen up to now. Recall first
that we divide the commands to the
computer into two categories, direct commands and program commands. We can set
them out as a table as follows: ⇨

Direct Commands	Program Commands
NEW	PRINT
RUN	INPUT
LIST	LET
	GOTO
	IF...THEN

Check on how well you understand
what they mean. NEW (or SCRATCH
on some computers) means to erase all of
RAM memory including any programs
or the contents of any variable locations.
When the NEW command is typed in
followed by pressing the RETURN key, all
the material you have entered, either
programs or responses to INPUT commands, are gone. The only way to have
defeated this equivalent of turning off
the power to the machine would have been
to save or store the program on some
mass storage device like a cassette recorder. You could prove to yourself that any
programs were gone after a NEW command
by typing LIST and pressing RETURN.
LIST commands the machine to print
out to the screen or the printer a complete
listing of any programs in RAM. If nothing is present in RAM, the computer will
respond to a LIST command by printing
READY or by a flashing cursor or both.
Type RUN and hit RETURN when you
want the computer to run or execute its
stored program. If you type RUN after

NEW, nothing will happen because there is no program left to run.

So much for the direct commands. The program commands all operate inside a program, although several of them can also operate as direct commands. For example, PRINT, followed by a literal string of characters inside quotation marks, will print that literal string on the next screen line. If a variable such as NA$ contained some symbols such as your name, then a direct command   ⇨

```
PRINT NA$
```

without any line number would immediately print the content of the memory designated as NA$ on the next line of the screen. But regardless of this secondary property of program commands, their major function is inside programs. One of them always occurs immediately after the program line number. A program line such as   ⇨

```
10 PRINT "HI, I'M YOUR
FAVORITE COMPUTER"
```

would execute by printing to the screen the message   ⇨

```
HI, I'M YOUR
FAVORITE COMPUTER
```

The PRINT statement is just a command to instruct the machine to print onto the screen or a peripheral printer the literal symbols in quotation marks following the command. Alternatively, the PRINT command can be used to print the contents of a memory location by a command such as   ⇨

```
50  PRINT XY$
```

which commands the machine to print the content of the variable XY$ to the screen. If the variable XY$ had been assigned the contents in line 30,   ⇨

```
30 LET XY$="NOW IS THE
TIME FOR ALL GOOD MEN"
```

then when the program reached line 50 it would have printed to the screen   ⇨

```
NOW IS THE TIME FOR
ALL GOOD MEN
```

Kids and Computers

If the variable XY$ were placed in quotes like ⇨

> 70 PRINT "XY$"

the output to the screen would be the cryptic ⇨

> XY$

The PRINT command also performs one additional important job. It evaluates arithmetic expressions. That means that if variable A=20, and variable B=15, the command ⇨

> 100 PRINT A + B

will print the sum, 35, on the screen. The other arithmetic operations, − (for subtraction), * (for multiplication instead of ×), and / for divide also are performed before they are printed. This line is a good example of how the PRINT command works. ⇨

> 200 PRINT A "×" B "=" A * B

This line will print to the screen the number stored in A, the symbol ×, the number stored in B, the symbol =, and the product of the numbers stored in A and B like this: ⇨

> 20 × 15 = 300

So the print command not only prints literals to the screen but also does calculations when numeric variables and operations are entered in a print line. Remember, if you simply want to print out literal symbols they must be surrounded by quotes; otherwise the print command interprets them as variables or operations.

In the preceding example we have given away the meaning of the program command LET. It is used for nothing more nor less than filling a variable name with some value from inside the computer program. For example, if we wanted a particular numeric variable, F1 to start life in a program with the numeric value 0, we would enter the line ⇨

> 1 LET F1 = 0

Later in the program we may choose to change the value of F1 by adding some number to it, say 4. In that case the command would be ⇨

> 90 LET F1 = F1 + 4

This shocking statement is just the kind of thing that makes the mathematically minded user shake. A mathematician of my acquaintance once remarked that if a computer accepts an equality like that, he knew why he did not like those machines. There is passing truth to his complaint; how could F1 = F1 + 4? The answer is that F1 is not a variable in the mathematical sense; it is simply the name of some storage compartment in the computer. Consequently, the relation = used in line 90 is not expressing an equality, rather it is merely a verb operating as an assigner of value. You may think of it as "becomes," because it signifies what F1 becomes. Line 90 could be translated as "let the number at memory location F1 be the content of F1 (i.e., 0) plus the number 4." The operation would leave the memory at F1 with a stored value equal to 4. If we looped back to this line later and line 90 executed again, F1 would become 8.

The program command INPUT is designed to permit variable assignment from the keyboard. The function of the command is exactly like LET, except that it permits the right half of the LET command after the equal sign to be entered from the keyboard. So if a program requires that information of an unknown kind fill a particular variable, then the line ⇨

> 120 INPUT F1

or ⇨

> 120 INPUT F$

would permit the operator to type in a number in the first case, or a literal string of letters or symbols in the second. Notice that the computer keeps track of the type of variable (string or numeric) that needs input. If you were to enter your name as input for F1, the computer might stop executing the program—a crash—and it would then print out an error message something like ⇨

```
TYPE MISMATCH ERROR IN 120
READY
```

The message READY printed by the computer means that the program is no longer being executed. In order to get it running again, you could retype RUN followed by RETURN. Some computers catch mistakes of this kind without interrupting the ongoing program. These machines print out a prompt message such as ⇨

```
REDO FROM START
?
```

that permits you to reenter the correct input. The INPUT command is a dangerous and occasionally touchy command. If a RETURN or ENTER command is pressed without entering any input, the computer may jump out of the program and signify that it has quit running with a READY. Most BASIC dialects permit you to restart such accidental halts by entering a direct command that continues the program from the point of departure. The usual syntax of this direct command is CONT, short for *continue*.

We have already seen how the GOTO command permits us to escape the tyranny of the line numbers. By entering a GOTO command, we may branch the program forward or backward to either get ahead to some advanced point or to return in the form of a loop to an earlier part of the program. Let us try to code such a loop to see how it would work. To print a message over and over again, you may recall that we needed code such as ⇨

```
5    PRINT "TYPE YOUR NAME"
10   INPUT NAME$
20   PRINT "HELLO ";NAME$
30   GOTO 5
```

This code would continue to repeat TYPE YOUR NAME, and after the name, say JANE, was entered it would print HELLO

JANE. The computer would then return to line 5 and print TYPE YOUR NAME. This loop would go on until you entered a BREAK from the keyboard or pressed RETURN with no input at the input prompt. If line 30 was changed from GOTO 5 to GOTO 20, once the program was started it would fill the screen with ⇨

```
HELLO JANE
HELLO JANE
HELLO JANE
HELLO JANE
HELLO JANE
HELLO JANE
[Etc.]
```

This bit of excitement would only stop if the BREAK key was hit. It is a neat program and one that kids enjoy showing to their friends. It is full of excitement and animation because it exhibits an interesting property of the computer screen called *scrolling*. Scrolling, you will recall from Chapter 4, refers to the fact that if information on the screen continues to be added, a new space is created at the bottom to accept the information, and the stuff on the current top line disappears from the top of the screen. And disappears means what it says. The information is gone.

Once a child has seen this program run, the child asks whether the screen can be filled with the printout of his or her name rather than just watching the print scroll down the left edge. The answer takes us to some formatting tricks that BASIC uses. Remember that the output of any computer goes to the screen in a simple, standard way. The term *output formatting* refers to the use of special code available in the BASIC programming language that lets you control how the print will be arranged on the screen or a printer. The two punctuation marks—the semicolon (;) and the comma (,)—are the simplest built-in formatters of the screen image. The semicolon serves to suppress a carriage return after a print statement. We used it between the literal "HELLO "

101

and the variable NAME$ so that they
would both print on the same line. The
comma serves a different purpose. It is
like a tab key on a typewriter with fixed
tab stops. If it is entered between print
statements, it tabs over to a new column
to start the next statement. Usually the
comma is set up to tab every 10 columns.
That means that this program   ⇨

```
10 PRINT "HELLO",
29 GOTO 10
```

will produce a screen display that looks
like   ⇨

```
HELLO HELLO HELLO HELLO
HELLO HELLO HELLO HELLO
HELLO HELLO HELLO HELLO
HELLO HELLO HELLO HELLO
HELLO HELLO HELLO HELLO
HELLO HELLO HELLO HELLO
HELLO HELLO HELLO HELLO
          [Etc.]
```

if your computer has a 40-column screen.
As the HELLOs get to the bottom of the
screen, the ones at the top scroll off
into the scrolling heaven. The program
generates an infinite loop, and consequently it can only be stopped by pressing the
BREAK key on the keyboard.

One of my students said, "I want to fill
the screen with my name, but I don't
want it to keep scrolling. How do I do
that?" Okay, remember LET F1 = F1 +4.
That made a memory location called F1
act like a counter that counted by fours.
Let us make one that counts by ones and
lets the program print until it fills the
screen. If the screen is 25 lines long and
we print in four columns, we will need
100 print commands to fill it up. Try
this: ⇨

```
 5 LET C = 0
10 LET C = C + 1
20 PRINT "ALICIA",
30 IF C = 100 THEN END
40 GOTO 10
```

Notice the comma after the name. Its purpose is to tab over to columns 10, 20, and
30 between each print of the name. Line

102

30 is the important one. It is our new IF . . . THEN command that permits the computer to make decisions. When this program is entered and the command is given to RUN, the computer evaluates the lines in the following way:

At line 5:
Open memory for numbers at location C; set C equal to 0.

At line 10:
Command that the number 1 be added to the current content; that makes C equal to 1.

At line 20:
Print the literal string of symbols, ALICIA, then move the (now invisible) cursor to column 10 and wait there.

At line 30:
Examine memory location C; if C equals the quantity 100, stop the program; if C equals any other number (any number!), go to the next line.

At line 40:
Go directly to line 10; do nothing else.

At line 10:
Add the number 1 to memory location C; that makes C equal to 2.

At line 20:
Print the string ALICIA, starting at the current cursor position (which is column 10) and then move the cursor to column 20.

At line 30:
Check C for 100; if C = 100, stop. If C> (greater than) or C< (less than) 100, go to the next line.

At line 40:
Go directly to line 10.

This exercise is what programmers call a *paper simulation*. It lets us check on what the computer will do at each line of the program. It is a useful tool for one of the programmer's major activities: *debugging*.

Computers are fairly clean devices, but they do get buggy. The *bugs* are what programmers call slips of the logical tongue that result in failures of the computer to behave as expected. If the failure is serious enough to stop the program, it is a CRASH. Much of the programmer's job is to find and eliminate bugs in the program. Consider the last program we wrote. If line 40 had sent the computer to line 20 instead of 10, we would be in an infinite loop. Instead of stopping after 100 prints, the machine would go on printing forever or until we pulled the plug. This kind of bug is fairly easy to find, as are misspellings of printed words. But some bugs are tough. Instead of stopping the program, they run beautifully. The only problem is that they give the wrong answers. If the wrong answers they give are fairly close to what a right answer would be, it may pass unnoticed. That is the dangerous bug.

A master statistician, a colleague of mine, had formulated a theorem that he could not prove, but if it were true it would be helpful for such tasks as predicting traffic snarls or nuclear power plant emergencies. He brought the formula to a friend with a big computer. The computer man said, "Not to worry, we can simulate the 200 billion tries on our computer in less than a month and see if the result conforms to your prediction. Four months later I ran into my downhearted statistician. "It bombed," he said. "I just got the news; not that I believe that machine, but what

can I do?" I heard nothing more about the problem until two years later, when the computer man remarked that they had just fixed a bug in their big simulation program. You guessed it; the statistician was right. The theorem is true. All's right with the world—now. The point is that bugs that give nearly right answers can be worse than no answer at all. The moral is to test every program in some simple way if possible to see that it gives the right answer to questions for which you know the right answer.

A quick review of the logical structure of programs we can write with our simple commands will firm up our understanding. First we recheck the direct mode commands we use to control the operation of the machine. These are the commands that do not need line numbers and are executed immediately when they are typed in and the RETURN key is pressed. They are LIST, to show the program, RUN, to execute it, and NEW, to erase the program currently in memory. These direct commands can be augmented by some of the program commands that are used as though they were direct commands. PRINT can be used without a line number as a direct command to print out the content of an already full memory location. For example, PRINT C would display on the screen the number contained at memory location C. If a program halts for some reason, we can use the direct command CONT to restart the program.

In program mode we have the commands PRINT and INPUT that are used to display information on the screen or to get information from the keyboard. The PRINT command can be used to print either literal strings contained between quotation marks or the contents of memory locations named by variable names such as BD$ which identifies a string variable, or J3 which identifies a numeric variable. Thus the program command ⇨

```
200 PRINT LX$
```

might result in a screen display such as ⇨

```
PLEASE ENTER YOUR EXPENSES
FOR LAUNDRY AND CLEANING
```

because the variable name LX$ was used to store this message, probably earlier in the program with a line such as ⇨

```
50 LET LX$ =
"PLEASE ENTER YOUR EXPENSES
FOR LAUNDRY AND CLEANING"
```

When printing the value of numeric variables, the PRINT command also performs appropriate calculations. For example, if the variable C equals 5 and G equals 10, the program line ⇨

```
70 PRINT C + G
```

will print the number 15 on the screen and not 5 + 10.

The LET command was used above in its usual form to load a variable. It also performs arithmetic if numeric variables are involved, as in ⇨

```
120 LET A = C + G
```

which will store the number 15 in the variable A, if C equals 5 and G equals 10. Like the LET command, the INPUT command also performs the logic of loading values into a variable. INPUT, unlike LET, gets its values from the keyboard rather than from a statement inside the program itself. Thus if you need to include information in a program that only the user knows, such as a telephone number, then some lines like ⇨

```
150 PRINT "ENTER YOUR
        TELEPHONE NUMBER"
160 INPUT TP$
```

will store your telephone number in a string variable named TP$. Notice that string variables can store numbers as well as letters; that is, they simply store *symbols*. You cannot use the telephone number in TP$ for any arithmetic or other numerical operations. If you wanted to do some calculations with telephone numbers it would have to be stored in a numeric variable with lines such as ⇨

```
150 PRINT "ENTER TELEPHONE
    NUMBER—NUMBERS ONLY
    NO SPACES OR OTHER
    SYMBOLS"
160 INPUT TP
```

The warning not to use spaces or other symbols tries to prevent the user from making an input mistake, such as typing in TR3-7251 or 222-3344. In the first case the variable will not hold letters; in the second case it will quit accepting input at the hyphen.

Getting information in and out of the machine and its variables is the fundamental mode of computer activity. That is the role of the commands LET, INPUT, and PRINT. The line numbers, so noticeable in all we do, control the sequence of command operations. Insofar as the task is in some sense *linear*, in that step 2 must always be performed after step 1, the line numbers are adequate to control the order of execution of the program. However, if it is necessary to branch from one set of operations to another and then perhaps back, branching commands are needed. A branch command enables the computer to deviate from the inevitable order of the line numbers. We need special program commands to do this. There are two distinct types of branch: the unconditional GOTO and the conditional IF...THEN. GOTO simply sends the program to some line number other than the next line. IF...THEN sets up a condition in the IF clause, which if true sends the program to the THEN clause, which can send it anywhere else or make it do anything else. For example, we could rewrite our counting program to use IF...THEN to return to the print statement, rather than halting the program. Look at this program: ⇨

```
 5 LET C = 0
10 LET C = C + 1
20 PRINT "GABRIELLE",
30 IF C < 100 THEN GOTO 10
40 END
```

Let us simulate a RUN as we did with the previous example:

At line 5   : Make C = O.
At line 10 : Make C = 1.
At line 20 :
   Print GABRIELLE and leave the cursor at column 10 (the comma, remember?).
At line 30 :
   Check to see if C is less than 100; if it is go to line 10.
At line 40 :
   The program will never get here until the conditional in line 30 fails.

Notice first that this program does exactly what the previous program did but with a different logical structure. This is probably the single most important point to be made in this chapter, namely that there are many ways to program the same activities of the computer. Some ways are superior to others for reasons of economy, requiring fewer lines of code and therefore less computer memory to do the job. Other programs that do the same thing may be better because they minimize our mistakes. Still others may be easier to write without bugs in the first place.

In this form of the name-printing program, for example, if somehow the value of C got to be larger than 100, the program would still stop. In the first form, since the IF clause checked only for "equals 100," if C got larger than 100, the program would loop, or repeat, forever, that is, it would keep printing out the name to the screen. It could only be stopped by turning off the machine or pressing the BREAK key. Most programmers would consider the second version superior for this reason alone. The point is that there are many ways to write the

same program. Look for the best way, even before you begin. We will see in Chapter 9 the sorts of aids and helps people have developed to simplify program writing, such as *flowcharts*, which are meant to improve the logic of programs by showing where the flow of the program may go astray.

Enough, you say, of these trivial examples! Is there something to program I can get my teeth into? Let us try an educational program for a child learning the multiplication tables. There are more commands we will learn later that could make things in this program simpler or more interesting, but we can get the flavor of an educational program this way.

You recall that a loop is a way to make the computer repeat some set of program lines over and over again. Loops are controlled by the IF . . . THEN statement, which sets a limit by a logical test on when to stop the loop. Any loop that has a specific job to do has to be controlled. The use of the conditional IF command to check on the status of a variable in the loop is one way for you to exercise program control over the loop. BASIC offers other ways (often simpler) to make a loop, and we will look at one of them in Chapter 9. But suppose we wanted to make a program that would print out a multiplication table so that your child could study it.

Kids and Computers

The multiplication table program can start by asking the child which times table he or she would like to study: ⇨

```
10 PRINT "WHICH TIMES TABLE
   DO YOU WANT TO STUDY"
```

This will print the appropriate prompting message to the screen. Notice we do not need to include a question mark because the next program line, which will be an INPUT line, will print its own question mark. Of course that question mark will be on the next screen line—unless—of course! Why not suppress the line feed with a semicolon? Good thinking. Rewrite line 10 as ⇨

```
10 PRINT "WHICH TIMES TABLE
   DO YOU WANT TO STUDY";
```

Notice the semicolon after the quotation mark. If it were inside the quote, it would print with the prompt. We do not want that; we want the semicolon to be a command: no line feed, please! Now line 20, the input line ⇨

```
20 INPUT T
```

which when it runs will print to the screen, ⇨

```
WHICH TIMES TABLE DO YOU
WANT TO STUDY? [   ]
```

The cursor, shown by the brackets [   ], will take its position from the question mark printed by the input statement and flash for an input number. If you accidentally entered a letter or word at this point, some machines might display ⇨

```
TYPE MISMATCH ERROR
IN LINE 20
```

or another equivalent error message to tell you that you had entered the wrong input. But typing in a number, say 6, would load the memory location T which the input statement reserved for numeric input. The program could then proceed to print out a title across the top of the screen commanded from line 30: ⇨

```
30 PRINT "TIMES TABLE FOR  ";T
```

which will print ⇨

> TIMES TABLE FOR 6

if 6 was the number entered. Be sure, right now, that you understand just why line 30 will print out this statement. If it is not clear, review it again until you see that the stuff inside quotes prints as it stands, whereas the stuff outside the quotes prints the content of the memory that is called or addressed by the variable name. Now it would be nice to skip a print line on the screen to leave some space between the title and the table. Do this by commanding PRINT with nothing following the command. This will force an empty line to the screen before anything else is printed. ⇨

> 40 PRINT

Now we need to get the table printed. Since we plan to print out the table from 1 to 12, we need a loop that will print a multiplication 12 times. Start with a counter that will count to 12, and add the print and calculating line 60: ⇨

> 50 LET C = 1
> 60 PRINT C;" × ";T;" = ";C * T
> 70 LET C = C + 1
> 80 IF C = 13 THEN END

Notice that in line 60 the computer multiplies numbers joined by the * and not by the ×. The symbol × is used as a multiply symbol in what is printed to the screen for the user. The actual multiplication is performed by the *. Line 70 adds 1 to the loop counter, and line 80 controls the loop. Line 60 is the operative line. It prints the value of C first, which on the first pass through the loop equals 1, and then prints the symbol × followed by the value of T, which we assume was 6, and then the symbol = followed finally by the evaluated expression C * T, which is equal to 6.

At line 70, C changes from 1 to 2, and line 80 checks to see if C = 13; since it does not, the program proceeds to line 90, ⇨

> 90 GOTO 60

and prints line 60 again with C this time equal to 2, and therefore C * T equal to 12. At the end of the program run, C will be 13, and the program will end after having printed out: ⇨

```
TIMES TABLE FOR 6
        1  ×  6  =   6
        2  ×  6  =  12
        3  ×  6  =  18
        •    •       •
        •    •       •
        •    •       •
       12  ×  6  =  72
READY.
```

Before we leave this introduction to BASIC programming, let us return to a topic that was mentioned in Chapter 6— subroutines. The ability to branch that is intrinsic to the IF . . . THEN command lets us draw on program segments that may be useful on more than one occasion in the program. For example, if a program requires that we often must answer a question by typing Y for *yes* and N for *no*, then to check which INPUT was typed could be done by a subroutine. At the point that the question was asked, the program would branch to some set of lines out of the present order. These lines might look like: ⇨

```
1000  PRINT "TYPE Y OR N"
1010  INPUT ANSWER$
1020  IF ANSWER$ = "Y" THEN
      GOTO 500
1030  IF ANSWER$ = "N" THEN
      GOTO 600
```

Lines 500 and 600 would be the start of segments of the program to take action depending on our answers. Without belaboring the point, subroutines make programming easier because a single piece of code can be referenced many times during the program run.

Programming Exercises

1. We write a program that asks for degrees Celsius and prints out degrees Fahrenheit. The formula is $F = 9/5 \times C + 32$

```
10   PRINT "ENTER THE CELSIUS TEMPERATURE";
20   INPUT C
30   PRINT "FAHRENHEIT TEMPERATURE IS "; (C * 9/5) + 32
```

Notice the semicolon after the prompt in line 10 and the space inside the quotes in the print statement of line 30. Also check that we put the multiplication and division inside parentheses. That is because we want to do this arithmetic before we add the 32. The computer could have handled this without the parentheses because it performs arithmetic in a standard order: multiply and divide first, add and subtract later.

2. Now we write a program to calculate a return on our investment based on yearly interest rates.

```
10    PRINT "HOW MUCH ARE YOU DEPOSITING";
20    INPUT D
30    PRINT "HOW LONG ARE YOU LEAVING";D;"FOR"
40    INPUT P
50    PRINT "WHAT IS THE YEARLY INTEREST (ENTER AS A ";
60    PRINT "DECIMAL, E.G. 14% EQUALS .14)"
70    INPUT I
80    LET C = 1
90    D = D + D*I
100   IF C = P THEN GOTO 130
110   C = C + 1
120   GOTO 90
130   PRINT "YOUR RETURN IS ";D
140   END
```

Lines 10, 20, 30, and 40 are old stuff by now. Lines 50 and 60 show that if you have a long prompting message you can put it on two separate PRINT lines and join them together by a semicolon. At line 80 we have collected the deposit D, the period P, and the interest rate I. We start a counter C at line 80 that will count by ones (see line 110) until it reaches P. Inside the counting loop, the current amount D will be added to D times the interest rate. When the period is reached, line 100 sends the program to line 130 for the final print and the end of the program.

Let us now turn our attention from programming, the software side of computers, to the hardware and the marketplace.

Chapter 8

How to Buy a Microcomputer

After completing Chapters 5 and 7 you may now consider yourself a genuine solid gold computer programmer, as well as chief computer supervisor of your child's computer education. As such, the bottom line quickly becomes, "Should we buy one?" The answer to this question is like a decision to buy a videotape recorder, a video disk player, or a high-fidelity system. But there is one important difference. Although the video and audio machines will provide hours of family entertainment and new video models may even offer interactive programs, none of them can be programmed by you or your child. Furthermore, they are intrinsically passive devices. Any interaction between your child and the television screen is powerfully constrained by the recording. Computers, even the game machines for playing video games, are a different kettle of fish. They have programs that modify their output as a result of input commands from the user. These input commands may be generated by a joystick on the video games rather than a keyboard, but they function exactly as though certain keystrokes had been entered from a computer.

If you can justify the cost of a video recorder or disk player in your family budget, you can probably afford a computer. Today's computers can be bought for less than $100, if you are willing to share your TV with the computer. But price alone is not sufficient to serve as the sole criterion for such a decision. Some hard thinking will have to take place, based on your intentions, your children's interest in such a project, and various imponderables in the expanding and rapidly changing hardware market.

The plan of our review of the most popular machines will be based on certain general requirements for any machine, as well as my experience in advising the parents of children at The Children's Computer School. These personal views reflect my analysis of the educational effectiveness of these microcomputers. In particular I am most concerned with the advantages and disadvantages for learning how to program presented by the current crop of machines. If other factors have an overriding importance for you, for example portability, then certain compromises may be required. The importance I assign to particular features results from my experience in teaching hundreds of kids to program computers. The list here, arranged in my own order of priority, reflects the options I believe must be considered by any parent who plans to purchase a computer.

Kids and Computers

1. Full-featured computer with optional peripherals or video game with no independent programming capabilities?
2. Key- or membrane-type keyboard?
3. Separate numeric keypad
4. True screen editing
5. Various mass storage options including cassette recorder and floppy disk
6. BASIC interpreter in firmware (ROM) or software?
7. Multiple programming-language capability
8. Color capability for use with color TV
9. Interface capabilities for modems or other special peripherals

Video games are the current craze among many youngsters. These games represent an application of microcomputer technology that has swept the world by storm. The reactions of people to these games are highly variable. In some countries, such as the Philippines, the coin-in-the-slot variety are outlawed. In some localities in the United States, parents are up in arms to stop the video parlors from operating. We have confronted this problem in meetings among our teachers and among the parents of children in The Children's Computer School. Many alternatives have been discussed. They range from parents strictly forbidding their children to play these games to moderate approval by some parents who feel that the games are a harmless (although costly) amusement. I would not condone such activity on the part of children who invest excessive amounts of time and money in the machines. Still, there is nothing intrinsically pernicious in such game playing, except that it may occupy more

time than other forms of entertainment. On the other hand, by several estimates, children currently spend about 25 hours a week watching TV, which seems a lot even for this often educational enterprise. Several parents of children in our school have come up with an acceptable alternative to the coin-operated games that appears to work. They offer to get a home machine that can be programmed with video games in return for contributions from their children of cash that would have gone into the video parlor slots.

The purchase of such a machine should be a family affair decided by a family discussion. The decision to buy a microcomputer should entail a review of the features, types, and prices of these machines. As a start, some visits to computer stores or other shops that stock home computers will give you an assortment of literature to use as a basis for comparison. With the burgeoning of computer manufacturers, sales outlets, and the media blitz that accompanies this activity there is small reason to wonder why this purchase decision is a complicated one. If you have made a trip to the retailers, you may have seen that part of the problem is that two distinct types of computer products are currently marketed, both of which may be thought of as home computers. These machines are the video game machines and the true home microcomputers. If your children's interests are fanned by the prospect of video games, you may think that the purchase of a game machine makes the most sense, especially since the price of game machines is (at the moment) somewhat less than the price of a home computer.

A strategy of this kind is only practical if there is no desire to enter this new world of programmable microcomputers.

Although game machines are computers, their input and output systems are restricted by their design. Some video game machines are supposed to become computers if keyboards or other components are attached to them. I find that, like any multipurpose device, they often do only their primary job well. Indeed, even the primary job is sometimes sacrificed to the needs of the multitude of other functions. Game playing can properly be an adjunct to an interest in the uses of a computer itself. My experience with students who not only play games but write game programs has convinced me that interest can grow regardless of its origins. However, if this principle is to operate at all, it means that you should purchase a home computer, not a video game machine. Please understand that the computer is, of course, the multipurpose device par excellence. But, unlike the "expandable" game-playing machines, the main parts of the microcomputer are fairly standardized. The broad utility and generality of the microcomputer is contained in the software, i.e., the programs.

The decision to acquire a microcomputer depends on your answers to a series of questions. First of all, many kids love computers, especially the idea of computers that they can use themselves. Some children, however, may not share quite this enthusiasm. For them the decision should probably be postponed. These children should first have the opportunity to use a computer at school or at special schools like The Children's Computer School. Sometimes parents say to me that their children have trouble with science and math and therefore maybe it is a bad idea to try to interest them in computers. From my perspective, not only will computers help these children, but as we have demonstrated at The

Children's Computer School, such children are often drawn out by the machines and the directly rewarding fun thay can have with them. As for bright and precocious children, the reasons to have a computer around for them is analogous to the reasons to have an encyclopedia. And, of course, you may find a home computer valuable for household uses, thus the machine dovetails into a multitude of needs and desires.

Once the decision to buy a microcomputer has been made, your attention should turn to features that are useful and desirable for you and your family. As you know, the first part of the computer you and your children will interact with is the keyboard. The keyboards on microcomputers divide into two major classes: membrane, or film, type and separate-key type. Each type comes in several different forms.

The membrane keyboards are a single and continuous sheet of soft Mylar plastic that is imprinted with a picture of a keyboard. If you touch the image of a key on this sheet, the computer reads that touch or press as though a real key had been depressed. Many people find keyboards of this kind annoying to use. However, some of these membrane keyboards give a "click" when a "key" is touched, and I find that this tactile feedback helps when using machines of this type. Many other people seem to have no difficulty with these keyboards. Sometimes it takes a while to get accustomed to them. Their main advantage is their price. They may reduce the cost of a computer by 10% to 15%. Occasionally this extra money is put into additional RAM memory, and therefore the prices of machines with membrane keyboards appear to be the same as those with separate keys.

A major advantage of the membrane board is that it is relatively impervious to spills or dirt and dust. There are no crevices between the keys for foreign matter to enter. This is quite important if the machine is to be used in a sandy or dusty area. It is also important if your children enjoy writing programs while eating a peanut butter and jelly sandwich. One quick swipe with a damp cloth after the session and the keyboard is as good as new. I have had computers of the separate-key type rendered inoperative by the failure of the RETURN key. The cause was a speck of dust on the contacts.

The second kind of keyboard is one with separate keys like the keys on a typewriter. There are two sorts of keyboards of this kind: the typewriter style that you find on the Radio Shack TRS-80 Model III or the Commodore VIC-20, or the calculator-type buttons that are used on the Texas Instruments TI-99 or the Radio Shack Color Computer. If most of your computer activities will be directed toward games, calculations, or other uses that do not require lots of keyboard entry, the calculator-style keys are fine. On the other hand, if you plan to get into word processing or other uses that require typing extensive letter inputs, a typewriter-style keyboard seems best.

Some keyboards have a special set of from 10 to 16 keys separated from the main keyboard. These keys are used for numerical entry. This *numeric keypad* is often regarded as a useful feature, especially if lots of number entries are anticipated. I also find that it is useful for game programs that two people can play, one using the regular keys for input and the other using the number pad. Finally, there are some machines that contain extra *user definable* or *soft keys* that can be programmed to do special input operations. Such soft keys can usually be simulated by appropriate programming so that regular

keys on the keyboard can perform special functions. However, it is convenient to have some keys that are undefined to begin with and that can be set up to do special tasks.

Once you have made the major choice between keyboards, the next move is to get as many extra features as you want or need. You are advised to do this because changing the keyboard (or adding a new keyboard) is both expensive and difficult. Get the keyboard you like to begin with. Try out membrane- and typewriter-style keyboards. If you like the membrane type, you can invest the money saved in more memory or other peripherals. As to separate key systems, I use the calculator button type for experimental setups in my laboratory. There it has the advantage of slowing down expert typists and requiring them to take care in entering the code symbols we use in our experiments. They make fewer mistakes in this kind of abstract keyboarding with a calculator-style keyboard. In general, used by the keyboard-sophisticated to enter words and for typing, the calculator-style keyboard generates more mistakes than the standard typewriter style.

A number pad is a useful feature, but remember that the Apple II, for example, does not have one and yet remains among the most popular home computers. I believe, however, that all the newer models including the Apple will provide a separate number pad, and, consequently, I am led to believe that it must be worthwhile or the manufacturers would not spend the additional money to include it on their new systems. If you anticipate using the computer for the entry of large quantities of numerical data, e.g., accounting and bookkeeping or statistical calculations and data analysis, then a separate number pad is a necessity. Some machines do not contain a separate set of keys as a number pad, but permit the redefinition of some keys as number keys. The Otrona Attaché and the Epson HX-20 have keyboards of this kind. These functional keypads, although not as convenient as a dedicated number pad, do help when lots of numbers have to be entered.

For myself, I would choose a typewriter-style keyboard with a separate numeric pad and additional soft keys. These keyboards are mostly present on the "high" end of the product lines. I would not sacrifice a peripheral mass storage system, for example, a cassette deck, to get such a better keyboard, but I would accept 16,000 bytes of RAM instead of 32,000 or 48,000 in order to get a better keyboard to begin with. After all, RAM memory is usually easy to add (but check this out on the machine you are interested in), and the programming you will be doing during your learning period will not require lots of memory. RAM memory is important when your programs require that the machine work with data that must all be present at the same time. If your data can be moved in and out of peripheral memory storage, you may spend a little more time at the computer, but you can save on the amount of RAM memory the computer requires.

All home computers except the pocket computers and some portable models use a video screen for their primary output. This video output is available in two forms: with a dedicated video monitor that is part of the machine itself or one that requires a connection to a separate video monitor or TV set. Obviously, the price of computers that attach to a monitor or your TV set should be, on the average, lower than those that are equipped with a video monitor of their own. Unhappily, this is not always the case. Some of the most popular machines require a sepa-

rate display. But notice that unless you use your own TV set, the cost of a separate monitor must be added to the total price. Microcomputers that connect to a TV usually offer the option of using color in the video display. Indeed, the Tandy Corporation Radio Shack model of this kind is called the Radio Shack Color Computer.

Some machines are monolithic with respect to the video display. That is to say, the video is an integral part of the computer itself, as for example, the Commodore PET® and the Radio Shack TRS-80 Model III. Other machines that are usually used with a dedicated video monitor, such as the IBM Personal Computer, permit a choice among such monitors. Sometimes an extra accessory called an *rf modulator* is included in the purchase price, either separate or built into the machine. The Radio Shack Color Computer has the rf modulator built in; the Commodore VIC-20 includes it as a small attachment. On some machines the rf modulator must be purchased separately before the computer can be connected to a home TV.

The advantages of a monolithic arrangement are that you avoid connecting cords and cables and the attendant problems such plug-in connections often generate. On the other hand, modularity and separability of components permit an arrangement of the computer's parts to satisfy individual tastes. In addition, if a component fails, that single unit can be removed for servicing. My own preference is for a monolithic machine with a dedicated video display, but some of the newer models that connect to the TV are very impressive. In general, I believe that if the microcomputer is going to be used by a single individual in the home, the monolithic "stand-alone" machine is preferable.

117

Kids and Computers

For classroom use the monolithic style is, in my experience, almost a necessity. Any cables or other connectors form a trap that is bound to spring just when a child has entered a long program in the machine. Also, if the video display is balanced on top of the machine, it is likely in the heat of programming to be toppled by a finger placed on a line to check the syntax. However, if care is taken in the design or purchase of adequate furniture that accommodates a separate video monitor, and has tunnels or special paths for the cables, then such a setup has several long-term advantages. Because it is modular, the components can be serviced, replaced, or upgraded individually. Also, one may interchange the style or features of the output from, say, black and white to color as desired. Under pressure from several of my instructors, I have even agreed to install such systems on an experimental basis for some of our courses at The Children's Computer School. For the youngest children in our 3R's program such systems will permit a creative use of color for teaching primary subjects. For our advanced programming students, these modular machines provide more flexibility in their operating systems and peripheral attachments.

If your family is planning to use the machine as part of an entertainment center, a unit that connects to the TV and has facilities for incorporating additional input controls such as joysticks is clearly preferable. Joysticks or other game control devices are merely an alternative input system that bypasses the typewriter keys and permits control of the computer's input by moving a control rod mounted on a small box.

Control devices like joysticks can be used not only for games but also for entering answers in computer-aided instruction programs and generally as an input

system where geographic or geometric direction rather than numbers or letters is the main element of the program input. Other input devices that can be attached to many personal computers include light pens, which when touched to the video display pick up information to use as input to the machine. Another kind of input device that you should know about is the graphics tablet. This is a flat plate and a stylus that together permit you to enter graphic or pictorial material into the computer. When the stylus is touched to the tablet, the computer reads the location of that touch and treats that spot as an input. Later, these inputs can be reassembled and used to draw a picture or graph of the input, or some programmed changes the machine did to the input.

Finally, there are input devices called paddle controllers that work like a joystick but consist of a knob that can be turned in one direction or another. Most of the current collection of microcomputers will accept these input systems, but some provide for easier connection than others. If you plan to use your computer with joysticks or paddle controllers, it is wise to make sure that your computer can accept these controllers easily.

All currently available computers provide for peripheral mass storage by cassette tape—the low cost route—or floppy disks. Your first mass storage system will probably be a cassette device, but you must make sure that adapting to a floppy disk drive will not create an unreasonable future expense. For most home uses a floppy disk is as much mass storage capability as is needed. If, however, your plans for your computer extend beyond home use, you may want to check that additional disk drives and possibly hard disk storage systems are also available.

Every computer needs a peripheral mass storage system. Not everyone needs a peripheral printer. You should be aware, however, that a printer attached to your computer will make learning how to program easier by letting you examine at your leisure the listing of the program. But connecting a peripheral printer to your computer can be complicated, especially if you want to connect one that is not made by the manufacturer of your machine. The primary reason for this complication is that computer printers (and other peripheral devices as well) conform to one of two quite different standards, or protocols, as they are often called. Furthermore, computers are often designed by their manufacturing engineers to encode their letters and numbers in idiosyncratic ways. The engineers do not do this to spite you; rather they are attempting to optimize the machine's performance at the lowest cost. This is why you may find that a

machine using some special protocol can write a million bytes to its floppy disk, whereas a competitive machine can write only 250K bytes to a similar floppy. The easy and most practical solution to this problem is to use a printer or other peripheral made by or recommended by the computer manufacturer.

Mass storage systems are often integrated into a computer, sharing the box that houses the CPU and memory or in the box that holds the video screen. Printers are normally connected by a separate cable even in these highly integrated machines. There are only two microcomputers that I know of that contain both a mass storage system and the printer in the same case as the computer. They are the Hewlett-Packard HP-85, and the Epson HX-20. The HP-85A is shown in Figure 30 and is only slightly larger than a portable typewriter. The HX-20 is even smaller and yet it contains the major

Figure 30: The H-P 85, a microcomputer that integrates the keyboard, the CRT, the printer, and mass storage on the tape cartridge that can be seen below the printer. (Photo courtesy of Hewlett-Packard Corp.)

components of an extensive computer system.

There are two ways to get your home computer to start accepting your programs in BASIC or in some other high-level language, that is, a language that uses English words for the program commands. First, the machine may have a BASIC interpreter stored in ROM. The ROM is, you will recall, the read-only memory that the computer uses for its own special purposes. The ROM retains information even when the computer is turned off. The RAM, or random access memory, is the storehouse for information that you enter into the computer. Information stored in RAM disappears when the power to the computer is removed. If the BASIC interpreter is stored in ROM, then when the machine is turned on, the BASIC programming language is immediately ready for you to use.

Some machines require that the interpreter program that makes the computer able to understand commands in BASIC—which is usually written in machine language, the computer's native tongue—must first be loaded into the machine from some mass storage system. A few machines have a small ROM with a tiny program that serves to load, or "boot-up," into RAM a high-level programming language. This bootstrap program in ROM requires only that you give a simple command to load up the BASIC interpreter. Some machines like the Otrona Attaché, make this ROM-based loader go to work when the machine is turned on. All you have to do is see that the disk or tape with the interpretive language is in position on the mass storage peripheral. These ROM-based machine language programs that attend to the housekeeping for the computer are aften called firmware because they are software stored in hardware.

These two ways to ensure that your computer be programmed in an easy-to-learn language like BASIC are both widely used by the industry. In earlier days, ROM memory was cheaper to manufacture than RAM, so most computer makers used ROM to store the needed interpreters. However, a RAM-based interpreter has the advantage that the programming languages are easy to change. They only require a new tape or disk to let you change the programming language from, say, BASIC to Pascal or FORTRAN. Either procedure is acceptable; however, the ease of use of a ROM-based BASIC may be overshadowed by the rich possibilities of booting a variety of programming languages into a large RAM. The original reason the advertisers gave for ROM-based languages was the "user friendliness" of the systems. Just turn it on and go! The most probable commercial reason was the higher cost of RAM memory compared to ROM. But today, RAM prices are dropping rapidly. Consequently, although I use a machine with a ROM-based language interpreter, when I replace my current microcomputer by trading it in for a new model, I may buy one that has all of its memory in RAM.

As we saw earlier, in Chapter 4, connecting peripherals to the computer is commonly an idiosyncratic arrangement. The major peripherals—mass storage systems like cassette decks or floppy disk drives, and printers to permit hard copy output—are the first upgrades you will add to your machine. Manufacturers use either their own system or some modification of a standard system. There are two major ways to do it. First, the peripheral connection can provide for information from the computer to dribble in and out in machine code one bit at a time. This method is called *serial communication,* because the stuff comes out in serial order—one bit follows the other. Remember that the bit, or binary digit, is the smallest unit of information. If the input or output to the computer is performed bit by bit, i.e., serially, the transmission rates are bound to be slower than if the system sends many bits at a time. Such a transmission scheme that sends many bits at once is called a *parallel port*, or *parallel interface*.

The current industry standard for the serial scheme is called *RS-232C*. The speed with which the bits are transmitted over the RS-232C connection is measured by a number called the *baud rate*. Bauds are like bits per second. Thus a baud rate of 300 is roughly 300 bits per second. Since each letter takes about one byte, or 8 bits, a 300-baud transmission will move about 40 characters per second. If your computer has such an RS-232C port, it can participate in serial communication. Because this method is usually slow, it is often supplemented or sometimes completly replaced by parallel ports.

This form of port sends its information in bunches, often 8 bits, or one byte, at a time. This parallel communication port can be as simple as a byte-by-byte transfer of data and control or a more complicated transfer of data and control at the same time. This more complicated way forms a standard called the *IEEE 488 standard*. Some machines can transmit and receive information from peripherals by both protocols. However, at the present time the only way to send your computer's talk over a telephone line is by an RS-232C port. If the computer only has a parallel port or an IEEE 488 port, you will need some sort of translator or interface between the computer's output and, say, the modem that connects to the telephone line. In my view manufacturers would be

well advised to include a built-in modem as a feature of their new machines. Then, a simple modular telephone cord would allow you to get on-line to central services such as CompuServe without additional gadgets.

With these preliminaries out of the way we can turn to a selection from the current crop of computers and consider them in some appropriate competitive categories. Sometimes a particular system should show up in more than a single category. When that happens I may remark on it, but the machine will not be listed again under the new category separately. The prime categories will be in terms of cost because, as a student of mine remarked, "When you don't have much to spend, you can waste a lot of time dreaming."

Obviously, I cannot identify every microcomputer in current production. There are more than 70 at this time. Many exceptional machines are produced by small manufacturers with limited sales, mostly for business and commercial use. Remember that you may find a machine such as the Intertec SUPERBRAIN on sale and a good buy, even though it is not included here. Your background from reading this book will make you a smart shopper, and you may even do better than the machines that I recommend in the following categories. I have restricted myself to popular and widely available machines, or to machines that have special or unusual features.

Category 1. The Pocket Computer

These machines are all quite small and thin. They look like a large pocket calculator but with many more keys. Figure 31 is a picture of the Sharp PC-1500 connected to its peripheral printer that also doubles as an interface for a mass storage cassette deck. This machine is almost identical to the Radio Shack TRS-80 Model PC-2 pocket computer.

Table 3

Pocket Computers

MAKE & MODEL	APPROX. PRICE	FEATURES
Casio FX820P	$200	
Panasonic H1000	$500	many peripherals
Quasar HK2500	$500	equivalent to Panasonic H1000
Radio Shack TRS-80	$280	
Sharp PC-1500	$275	equivalent to TRS-80 above

The enormous advantage of these machines is their extreme portability. Their main disadvantages are their output displays, which show only 20 to 30 characters of an 80-column line of symbols, and their keyboards, which are small by necessity. In order to see all the remaining characters in a program line for example, it is necessary to scroll the display. These computers have one important feature that will shortly be used in several larger machines. They all possess a special memory called a *CMOS chip* that functions as a RAM but retains its information with only a slight

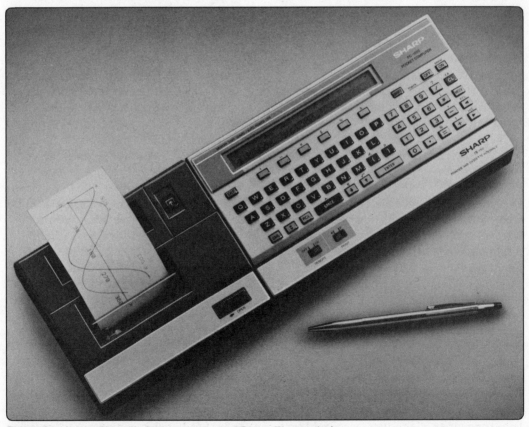

Figure 31: Sharp PC-1500. (Photo courtesy of Sharp Electronics)

Table 4

Portable Computers

MAKE & MODEL	APPROX. PRICE	FEATURES
Hewlett-Packard HP-85	$2400	includes printer and mass storage
Osborne 1	$1800	2-disk, no print, software
Otrona Attaché	$3500	2-disk, no print, software
Epson HX-20	$ 795	liq-crystal 4-line screen, printer

drain on the internal batteries. This means that a program loaded into CMOS RAM remains there until replaced or erased, even when the computer is switched off. All these machines have a ROM-based BASIC interpreter. They all can be connected to various peripherals for mass storage and printing.

If no reference to features is made, this reflects the fact that while all have peripherals, some have more than others. The price range of these machines is probably temporary and depends mostly on the current availability of business-useful peripherals for the Panasonic and Quasar machines. If you need this very small type of machine for its special virtue of portability, the Radio Shack TRS-80 PC-2 offers widely available sales and service. On the other hand, the broad range of peripherals for the Panasonic and Quasar machines make them suitable for many business and commercial purposes. These are not practical machines on which to learn to program, because they use small keyboards which are difficult to use without practice. The lack of a large screen display means that editing and debugging may be a real chore.

Category 2. The Portable Computers

There are currently several computers that are called portable, although all microcomputers can be more or less easily carried. To be a portable, the computer, the screen, a mass storage system, and maybe even a printer are integrated into something you can carry as easily, say, as a portable typewriter.

The first, and most honestly a portable is the Epson HX-20. This machine, which has a full typewriter keyboard, also contains a built-in printer, and may be fitted with a microcassette recorder for mass storage. Its portability is defined by the fact that it is battery powered, and so can be used anywhere. Its only real limitation is the display, which is a liquid crystal 4-line by 20-column arrangement. Although it will scroll over a longer and wider "page," it is still a limitation for uses that require a more extensive display, and obviously, this machine is not for game playing. Indeed, I think it would be greatly improved if the inadequate printer were eliminated and the screen enlarged to perhaps 4 lines × 80 columns.

The Osborne 1 comes "naked," that is, without an operating system in ROM. You will recall that without such a ROM-based interpreter you must load such a system from a mass storage peripheral. Because the Osborne 1 comes complete with two floppy disk drives as its mass storage system, one of the two disk drives in the unit can be used for this purpose. As a result of this design decision the Osborne 1 has a comfortable 64K of RAM as standard. This machine comes complete with business software to do things like word processing and spread-sheet modeling.

The HP-85A, on the other hand, has BASIC in ROM, which means it is ready to program as soon as you turn it on. The machine comes with 16K of RAM as a user work space to which an additional 16K can be added by a plug-in module. This computer has fantastic numeric computational ability and super graphics. It can be programmed to draw quite complex engineering and scientific graphs. This is a product of the long experience Hewlett-Packard has had in the design of engineering calculators and general scientific equipment. The HP-85A can also be connected to a host of peripherals through its IEEE 488 port.

The third portable is the Otrona Attaché which, at almost twice the price of the Osborne, is in quite a different class. For the business or professional user, its graphics and screen resolution may make it the selection of choice. For the family it is much more than you or your children need for learning about and using a microcomputer. But if you consider it a machine primarily for work, and then bring it home for the family, it is hard to beat. I have used one for the past several months, and find its features and power very practical.

The choice here is easy. If you need a machine that can be transported easily for use at work and at home, then for business types of use the Osborne, the Otrona, or other portables and a separate printer at perhaps $600 for a dot matrix type may work well for you. For science and technology, and in particular the handling of numerical data, the H-P machine may be the best in the business, portable or not. For bigger numerical analysis in a not-quite-so-portable system the HP-85A has a big brother for the tabletop, the HP-86 with the potential (through plug-in modules) of half a million bytes of memory.

Category 3. Under $600

All but one of the computers in this category are designed to be connected to a (color) TV set. Consequently, they can do various things with color by augmenting their standard BASIC with additional commands usable in both direct and program modes. The color of the background and the output to the screen can be controlled with these commands. These machines also accept various ROM-based programs that simplify program operation and add memory for large programs. The keyboards on these machines, except for two, are not like typewriter keyboards. I personally find this limiting in any applica-

Table 5

Computers under $600

MAKE & MODEL	APPROX. PRICE	FEATURES
Atari 400	$300	film keyboard, game cartridges
Commodore MAX	$150	film keyboard, game cartridges
Commodore VIC-20	$200	game cartridges
Commodore 64	$600	64K RAM
Radio Shack Color Comp.	$300	16K RAM; extended BASIC, add $100
Timex Sinclair 1000	$100	film keyboard; small, but expandable, memory
Texas Inst. TI99/4A	$400	calculator keyboard, LOGO available

tions of the home computer beyond games.

In this group I think that all the machines are worth considering. I would rank the first three as Commodore VIC-20, Radio Shack, and Atari. The Atari keyboard is the prime reason I rate it last, because it is a beauty as a teaching system; in the 800 version I think it may even outpace the Apple II. In addition it is unquestionably the best for color graphics on a color TV, but again, if I bought an Atari it would be the 800. The Radio Shack Color Computer is a fine system for educational and game use. To my mind the calculator-type keyboard limits its general use as a business machine. If you do pick the TRS-80 Color Computer, you should seriously consider buying it with Radio Shack extended BASIC, which adds $100 to the price.

The Texas Instruments TI99/4A is a color computer that is extremely popular for young children who use it with LOGO, a programming language that concentrates on the development of geometric ideas. The TI99/4A can also run software available in ROM-based cartridges and can be programmed in BASIC with a ROM-based interpreter.

The Timex Sinclair 1000 is the least expensive way to get into personal computing and except for the difficulty in using its nonstandard-sized keyboard, it can teach you a great deal about programming. It is clearly more than a toy, and for less than $100 it is a powerful but inexpensive introduction to computer programming.

The Radio Shack machine has one feature the other manufacturers should copy. There are no external boxes or oversized plugs and power supplies to interfere with your setup. Just plug the power cord into the wall, and plug the TV cord into the socket in the rear. The Commodore machines have these ungainly attachments connected to them, but they

also have a real typewriter-style keyboard, memory expansion capabilities, and a host of useful and powerful peripherals. Either the VIC-20 or the 64 is an excellent machine for getting into computers, both for programming and for other uses. They are machines that can keep up and even stay ahead of your needs. The Timex Sinclair 1000 is an ingenious device, although to my mind it is primarily of value for learning to program. As you know, I consider this to be the single most important aspect of computer literacy, and consequently this machine is, at its price, particularly worthwhile. But if there are other things you plan to do with your computer, the Timex may not be able to keep up. The Texas Instruments TI99/4A is potentially the most powerful of the group, but its packaging is not helpful for uses other than those that use the ROM-based programs that TI sells for it. It does possess one feature of importance. As I remarked previously, if LOGO programming capability is desired, the TI99/4A can be converted easily into a LOGO machine by a plug-in ROM cartridge. This is not the only machine that will accommodate a LOGO interpreter, but it is the best. Its graphics features are highly compatible with LOGO's geometric bias.

All these units require a separate cassette recorder for mass storage. These cassette units vary in price depending on the machine you buy, from perhaps $25 for a tape recorder to use with a machine like the Timex Sinclair to $65 for the special cassette recorder the Commodore machines require.

Category 4. $1000 and over

These are the big guns in the microcomputer department. These machines, along with the high-end portables, represent the current state of the art in general-purpose computers. Although I say general

Table 6

Computers over $1000

MAKE & MODEL	APPROX. PRICE	FEATURES
Apple II Plus	$1600	
Apple III	$3000	1-disk and 128 RAM
Atari 800	$1100	
Commodore P128	$1000	128K RAM, CRT extra
B128	$1700	128 RAM, monolithic
BX128	$3000	256K RAM, monolithic, 2-disk
Franklin ACE 1000	$1500	Apple II Plus compatible
Hewlett-Packard HP-86	$1800	64K RAM, needs $800 disk
IBM Personal	$1600	separate keyboard, CRT extra
Radio Shack TRS-80 III	$1000	monolithic
Zenith Z-89	$2400	monolithic, available as kit

purpose, they all have a strong bias toward business applications. The under $600 group are seen by their manufacturers as the entry-level machines for the home market. But these up-market machines, especially the low-end Commodore and Radio Shack units, have the capability for serious professional use while managing to stay in the consumer ball park with prices close to videotape recorders. I include the IBM Personal Computer and the Apple III in this group even though when appropriately configured with a video monitor they get into price ranges that probably exceed home computer budgets. I also consider the HP-86 in this class. Although unlike the Apple or the IBM, it cannot use a cassette machine as a simple mass storage system. In order to save and recall material from mass storage it is necessary to buy at least a single mini-floppy disk drive. This is a fair-sized investment itself and would just about pay for another computer. Most of the machines can use a monochrome video display, although the Atari, the Apple, and, with an optional feature, the IBM, can display color. If color is your interest, either for graphics or other uses, then the Atari may be your machine. All the machines in this group except the Apple II Plus and the Atari have a separate number pad on the keyboard, although the new Apple III has included this keyboard feature.

With an investment at this level it is important to ensure a source of service and support for your purchase. This point is central to a discussion of price in the home computer market. The prices I have quoted are approximations of retail price for roughly similar capabilities or are the minimum available prices for these machines as they are configured by the factory, e.g., the Apple III, which comes with a built-in disk drive and 128K of RAM. If these figures suggest that Radio Shack and Commodore prices are low, while Apple, Franklin, IBM, and H-P prices are high, that is a correct conclusion. This price difference represents essential differences in design philosophy. The Apple, the Franklin, and the IBM, for example, contain relatively costly expansion slots for installing a variety of peripherals, whereas the Commodore and Radio Shack machines are "buttoned-up" and not designed for the user to open up and fool with. A decision you must make is whether you need this additional capacity or want to pay for it in the expectation that you will need it. Are you a tinkerer? If so, get a machine you can modify on the inside like the Apple II Plus or the Franklin. Do you want to prevent little fingers from taking your computer apart? Get one that stays locked up.

But back to the service issue. With machines of this level of sophistication you will shortly be in the market for disk drives and printers. Indeed with the Apple III and the HP-86 you will be in that market immediately. Even though the computer is intrinsically reliable, these other components have mechanical parts that are bound to require service. If you shop around, you can find most of the machines in this list discounted from 15% to 25%, usually from mail order firms. The majority of these dealers are conscientious and responsible business people. But for these discounted prices they cannot offer personal service. Insofar as the manufacturers all provide some form of limited warranty, you can always get service by returning the machine to the maker. Most of us, however, would rather talk to our dealer and get advice and service from the seller. This means that you should expect to pay close to the retail price for this convenience, but be sure you can get what you're paying for by asking the dealer to let you see the service shop. A service guarantee without a repair facility is a joke. This is why Radio Shack is so successful. Carry-in service at a Radio Shack store is an enormous advantage to the customer, who needs to do nothing but drop off the component.

The nature of microcomputers begs for a solution to their service problem by a simple change in engineering and manufacturers' attitudes. The service departments that maintain these machines are supplied by the manufacturers with software that diagnoses trouble when it occurs, and that points to the chip or circuit card that needs to be replaced. If these diagnostics were delivered to the customer, service would amount to running the diagnostic program and snapping in a named replacement part. Simple color coding would make repair as easy as changing a light bulb.

As far as features and convenience are concerned, all these top-flight machines offer various advantages and disadvantages in use. Some have complicated or inconvenient editing features. Others have keyboards whose feel is not right. Most use dedicated video displays, but those that depend on your TV or a TV that you buy for the machine may offer less than adequate screen images when used with poor-quality TVs. Some of these machines restrict the number of screen columns (i.e., line length) to 40 characters, which is fine for many purposes, but not so good for word processing, for example. For this use, 80 characters per line is a pleasant if not necessary feature. Some of these high-level machines still do not offer both upper- and lowercase print as a standard feature. If you plan to use the machine for text work, you may need this capability.

I would be happy with any of these machines, but as you already know I prefer to eliminate connections and plugs, so a monolithic machine is my preference. As a machine for home use that would be used primarily to learn to program, your child would do well with any machine in this category. Indeed all of these computers are "system" microcomputers. They all accommodate much more memory than is needed for household chores, instructional programs, or learning to program. The extra memory is not necessary for most of the things for which we will use the computer. Remember that you can (and will) load and unload pieces of what you are doing from mass storage. The system works faster if more information is on-board and addressable by the CPU, but it is no smarter.

Among the modular machines, I would consider first the IBM Personal Computer, recognizing that it is a new machine and probably has some bugs in it and that in its finally configured cost it is bound to be a high-end purchase. I think, however, that I would wait until IBM fixes the seriously misplaced shift key before purchasing this machine. But on the whole, when you buy in this league you really cannot make a bad decision.

If you plan to use your machine mostly with software that you buy, a purchase decision should consider the software available for the machine. From this position the machine that offers the widest choice in preprogrammed software is the Apple II Plus and, of course, the Franklin ACE 1000, which uses the identical software. These machines are also extremely popular with people who plan to interconnect their computer with other systems for use as a controller or monitoring device. In the home such uses include attending to heating and cooling and to burglar and other intrusion alarms.

In the factory or business, the computer may control various manufacturing or monitoring functions. The easy access to the machine's interior in the Apple II Plus and the Franklin, and the provision of slots into which additional circuits can be installed by you, has given small manufacturers of such custom circuit boards a large market. These manufacturers provide a variety of accessory systems that can convert the basic Apple or Franklin into a customized system for specific technical jobs.

With this veritable smorgasbord of choices you may be immobilized by the vast diversity of options. As you conclude this chapter, bear in mind that any choice is likely to be a good one. The important thing to do, if you have a mind to, is to get started. One feasible alternative to committing yourself almost blindly to this purchase decision is to go to a computer school for an introductory hands-on course with microcomputers. Another possibility is to attend computer flea markets that are held in many cities. Finally, there may be an amateur microcomputer club that you can join or visit to hear about various machines from people who use them. Again, remember that the likelihood of a serious mistake in the low-priced market is small, but the return for you and your children, even with a minimal machine, is bound to be large.

Note: All prices are current as of December 1982.

Chapter 9

More Programming for Children

As your programming skill advances, you will be able to solve more difficult problems with your computer. In this chapter we will look at some aids for this task, as well as other tips to help your programs. What we discuss here will be most valuable if you have already taken our advice in the last chapter and now own a microcomputer. For those of you who have not yet started down the royal road to computer romance, the tips and hints in this chapter will serve all sorts of general purposes; perhaps they will even motivate you to sit down with your family to discuss a computer purchase. Remember, even if programming does not interest you, others in the family may become interested in the work just from your discussions and descriptions. This happened to the father of one of our students. He took our adult course but decided not to continue to program. Out of a sense of duty, the mother took the adult course so that she could encourage her son in his computer activities. After one and half years of course work she became a first-rate programmer and now contributes programs to the local computer club.

Since repetition with enhancements is a sensible way to imprint information, we review again the direct and program commands covered so far. Recall that

direct commands can be typed into the computer from the keyboard without line numbers, and they will execute as soon as the RETURN key is pressed. The *program commands* control the computer during a program run. They must be preceded by line numbers, and they execute only after the direct command RUN has been entered. This list is more complete than the earlier one because we have included commands for program file management (LOAD and SAVE), as well as some new commands we have not yet examined.

BASIC COMMANDS	
Direct	**Program**
NEW	PRINT
RUN	INPUT
LIST	LET
CONT	GOTO
SAVE (STORE)	IF . . . THEN
LOAD (CLOAD)	END
(PRINT)	
(GOTO)	

Notice that the list includes as direct commands PRINT and GOTO. We have already spoken about the use of PRINT as a direct command, but GOTO can also function this way. Indeed, the direct command GOTO followed, of course, by a line number permits you to start a BASIC program from line numbers other than the lowest, which is what the command RUN does.

These commands should be old friends by now. Therefore we will extend your growing knowledge of BASIC by introducing you to a different kind of code that is often used in BASIC programs. You will probably recognize some of these terms and the things they do, but now we will attend to them in greater detail and explain them more fully. These new objects of programming are called *functions*. For our purposes they divide into two main categories: logical functions and mathematical functions. First we shall list them and then we shall explain them.

BASIC FUNCTIONS	
Logical	**Mathematical**
AND	+
OR	−
NOT	*
<>	/
<=	↑ or ^
>=	SQR( )
<	(TRIG)
>	(LOG)
=	RND(1)
	TAB( )
	(STRING)

Let us start with the simple math functions; $+$, $-$, $*$, and $/$ are the symbols used for the usual arithmetic operations of addition, subtraction, multiplication, and division. The asterisk (*), as we learned in Chapter 7, is the multiplication sign that is used by all computers instead of the $\times$, to prevent ambiguity. The slash (/) is used to represent division. For example, 12/4, which evaluates to 3. Thus if the

direct command PRINT 12/4 was typed in, the machine would display the number 3 on its screen. The logic functions do almost exactly what they say. They are used to help an IF . . . THEN make a decision. For example, entering IF A = 3 AND B = 4 THEN PRINT "OK", would cause the computer to print OK only if A did equal 3 and B equaled 4. Both A and B have to be correct as stated for AND to let the conditional get to the THEN part. OR acts the same, except that OK would print if only one part of the IF were true. NOT just changes the truth of something, as IF NOT A = 5 THEN . . . would do the THEN part only if A did not equal 5. The symbols <>, <=, and >= mean "not equal to," "less than or equal to," and "greater than or equal to." We have already met =, equal to, <, less than, and its partner >, greater than, in Chapter 7.

The remaining mathematical operations and functions are useful in programs that compute with numbers. In most of the programs we will use to demonstrate programming methods, we will not be using these operators. The ↑ or ^ means "to the power of." The code PRINT 5↑2 would evaluate and print to the screen the number 25, which is the square of 5. Since SQR is the square root function, PRINT SQR(25) would print the number 5. Notice that this "spelled out" function requires that parentheses be used around the expression that is to be operated on. The trigonometric functions that most microcomputers contain are SIN, the sine function, COS, the cosine function, and TAN, the tangent function. These functions also require that the number or expression to be worked on (called *argument* by mathematicians) be enclosed in parentheses. Some microcomputers have two logarithmic functions, LOG (to the base 10) and LN (to the base e); others only have one. They also require that their arguments be placed in parentheses.

The RND, or random function, is probably a new one to you, even if you are familiar with log and trig functions from high school. PRINT RND(1) will, in many microcomputers, print a decimal number, e.g., .86325147, between 0 and 1. The next time the RND function is called you will get a new decimal. Each time the computer reads this command and function it will generate a new random decimal, that is, one that you could not predict. This function permits the computer to generate random numbers for use in games or other programs where something unexpected is required to happen. The random function is very useful not only to draw cards for a poker game but also to use to simulate or mimic various kinds of business possibilities. The TAB function is an easy one to use. When it follows a PRINT command, it moves the cursor before printing as many spaces to the right as are entered between the parentheses.

The functions we have called *string functions* are grouped together. They are used to manipulate strings of symbols. From our point of view they are some of the most important functions that a programmer uses. They are the operators that make the computer a general-purpose information processor, rather than a calculator. For example, one important string function is LEN( ). When this function is evaluated, it returns the number of letters in the string variable inserted in the parentheses. That is, LEN counts the number of letters or other symbols in the string variable. So if NA$ = "EUGENE" then LEN(NA$) will equal the number 6, because there are six letters in the name Eugene. This means that the little program ⇨

```
10 LET NA$ = "EUGENE"
20 PRINT LEN(NA$)/2
30 END
```

131

when the RUN command is given, will print the number 3 on the screen. Be certain that you know why this is true. Notice in particular that LEN(NA$) is not only a number but is one that can be operated on by mathematical functions. Other string functions that are found in many micro-computers include functions that cut up strings of symbols in various ways. The command PRINT LEFT$(NA$,2) will print the letters EU, while
PRINT RIGHT$(NA$,3) will print the letters ENE. The string functions make neat tricks possible. For instance, if you want to center the printing of your name on the screen you could code: ⇨

```
10  PRINT "TYPE YOUR NAME"
20  INPUT NA$
30  PRINT TAB(20 − LEN(NA$)/2)
    ;NA$
```

The number of spaces to be tabbed is (20 − LEN(NA$)/2). This is because the screen is (we assume) 40 characters wide. Half the screen width, i.e., the center of the screen, is at column 20. But if we started printing there, your name would run from the center of the screen to the right. To get it centered, we want to start printing half the number of letters in your name to the left of the center of the screen which is 20. Therefore, we subtract half the number of letters in your name, LEN(NA$)/2, from 20 to get the value of the tab.

This little program points out another important feature of your computer that we mentioned before. The computer performs mathematical functions in a specific order. In particular, it first divided the number of letters in your name, LEN(NA$), by 2 before it subtracted that number from 20. This occurs because the order of doing arithmetic is

1. Perform the operations inside parentheses first.
2. Raise to a power or take a root.
3. Multiply or divide.
4. Add or subtract.

This means that the operation   ⇨

> PRINT 40 − 2 * 10

will print 20 to the screen and not 380. If we wanted the computer to print 380 as the answer, we would need to enter the command as   ⇨

> PRINT (40 − 2) * 10

A final string function is MID$(A$,B,C). This function picks out the middle part of the string to be analyzed (A$ in this definition), starting at the B letter and proceeding for C letters. For example, if NA$ = "GABRIELLE", the command PRINT MID$(NA$,6,3) would print ELL, and PRINT MID$(NA$,3,4) would print BRIE. Notice that MID$ can do everything LEFT$ and RIGHT$ can do. LEFT$ and RIGHT$ are examples of useful but redundant commands.

Now we are ready to try something really fancy. Suppose we had entered a list of names. Do not ask how just yet; simply agree that there is such a list. Now we would like to print the list out with the last name first. To solve this problem, we must first agree that an adequate definition of a last name is the string of symbols following the last blank space. Sometimes this definition is inappropriate, for example, in a name such as "del Bello." But again for our purposes let us agree that the definition is close enough. We need a program that takes our name string apart letter by letter starting at the last letter and checks each one to see if it is a blank space. If it is, the program prints out the letters after the blank space.

Let us start by recognizing that to look through the letters of the name requires that we make a loop. This means we need to count up our passes through the loop, looking at a single letter each time through the loop. We begin by assuming that the name is stored in the variable location N$ and that the name is JOHN SMITH. So the coding should start this way: ⇨

```
10 LET C = 0
20 LET L = LEN(N$)
```

These two lines set up our working variables, our counter C and the length of our name string L. At line 20, C will be equal to 0 and L will be equal to 10 because:

```
 1 - J
 2 - O
 3 - H
 4 - N
 5 - (space)
 6 - S
 7 - M
 8 - I
 9 - T
10 - H
```

Now we search through the name string for the space: ⇨

```
30 IF MID$(N$,L − C,1) = " "
   THEN GOTO 60
40 LET C = C + 1
50 GOTO 30
```

The first time the program reaches line 30 it will check to see if MID$(N$,L−C,1) is equal to the space character. The string that line 30 finds will be the one letter (,1) at the tenth (L − C = 10 minus 0) position of the string N$, that is, the letter H. Because H does not equal a space the program will proceed to line 40, where C will be set to 1. At line 50 the program will switch to line 30 and check the one letter at position (L − C) which is now equal to 9 and will find the letter T which is also not equal to a space. At line 40 again, C will change to 2 because 1 + 1 is indeed 2, and at 50 the program will go to 30 to evaluate the new L − C letter, the letter I. Three more times around the loop will set C equal to 5, and now line 30 will evaluate MID$(N$,5,1) as equal to the space. With the IF clause true, the THEN clause will send the program to line 60, which reads ⇨

```
60 PRINT RIGHT$(N$,C)
```

134

which will print SMITH to the screen.
Whew! What a job, but you should note
that the whole business took the computer
about a tenth of a second.

If we put the whole program together,
we can see the structure of a loop. You
recall that a loop is a way to make the
computer repeat some set of program
lines over and over again. In this program
the loop was used to search for a particular
symbol in a string, the blank space before
the last name. ⇨

```
10 LET C = 0
20 LET L = LEN(N$)
30 IF MID$(N$,L − C,1) = " "
   THEN GOTO 60
40 LET C = C + 1
50 GOTO 30
60 PRINT RIGHT$(N$,C)
70 END
```

Let us extend the educational program
we developed in Chapter 7 for a child
learning the multiplication tables. Now we
will design a program to test and evaluate the ability of the child to do multiplication problems. Although we do not
extend this program to calculate test
scores, we can get the flavor of the
educational testing program: ⇨

```
10 PRINT "WHICH TIMES TABLE
   DO YOU WANT"
20 INPUT T
30 LET M = 1
40 PRINT M; "X"; T; "= ?"
```

Stop for a moment to get our bearings.
Line 10 prompts for a number which is
input at line 20 into the variable named T,
a numeric variable because it does not
end with $. Let us suppose the child
entered 8. Line 30 sets M, our multiplier
variable, to a value of 1. Line 40 prints
the message containing the number 1,
which is what M equals, the symbol X,
the number 8 (that is T, remember), and
the symbol =?. So the whole line on
the screen looks like ⇨

```
1 X 8 = ?
```

Now we need an input variable to get our
answer; let us use A: ⇨

```
50 INPUT A
```

When the child types in the answer and
presses the RETURN key, the memory
location named A fills with the number
that was typed in. Now we need to check
whether the answer is right or not, that
is, whether A is equal to M times T.

Kids and Computers

We could ask whether it is correct or whether it is not correct. From my experience I know that it will be easier to program if we check to see if it is wrong. When you see the rest of program you will also see the point of that checking procedure. Now we test the answer at line 60: ⇨

60 IF A <> M * T THEN GOTO 40

Line 60 checks to see if A is not equal to M times T. If the answer is not correct, the program reprints the problem by going back to line 40 and waits for a new input for A. If A does equal M times T, the . . . THEN command is not completed and the program falls through to line 70, which changes M to M + 1, then goes to line 80, and then line 40 and prints a new problem: ⇨

70 LET M = M + 1
80 GOTO 40

At this point the program will work all right, but it will never stop. To get control of the loop, we need another IF . . . THEN statement before line 80: ⇨

75 IF M = 13 THEN GOTO 10

The whole program then, in the correct order, is: ⇨

10 PRINT "WHICH TIMES TABLE
    DO YOU WANT"
20 INPUT T
30 LET M = 1
40 PRINT M; "X"; T; "= ?"
50 INPUT A
60 IF A <> M * T THEN GOTO 40
70 LET M = M + 1
75 IF M = 13 THEN GOTO 10
80 GOTO 40

The symbol X only stands for the letter x. It is used in the program merely as a symbol, because a child may not yet know about the * sign for computer multiplication. Do notice that the computer checks to see if M equals 13, and not 12 in line 75, because if it checked for a 12 the program would never print ⇨

8 X 12 = ?

Instead, after printing out 8 X 11 = ?, M would jump to 12 at line 70, and pass the test at line 75 and so jump back to line 10 before asking the 8 X 12 question.

The program that searched for the last name when we typed in a full name was only a demonstration. At that point we slid over how a lot of names would be entered or retained in a program. Now it is time to grasp this problem, one of the most difficult and abstract ideas in either programming or mathematics. The cocktail party names for these new kinds of variables, which are different in kind from string or numeric variables, are (catch your breath!) *vectors* and *matrices*. Hi ho, you just knew we would get to unfathomable mathematics. But not so! These fancy names are just jargon for what we would call lists and tables. A list is a vector, a table, like a multiplication table, is a matrix. That's not so bad, is it?

How could you get a list into the computer? Suppose it was just a grocery list such as:

1. Orange juice
2. Coffee
3. Corn flakes
4. Milk
5. Canned spinach
6. Mustard

One crude way to get it into the computer would be to write a program such as: ⇨

```
10  PRINT "ENTER LIST"
20  PRINT "WHEN FINISHED
    ENTER 'END'"
30  INPUT A1$
40  IF A1$ = "END" THEN END
50  INPUT A2$
60  IF A2$ = "END" THEN END
        •
        •
        •
4690  INPUT Z9$
4700  IF Z9$ = "END" THEN END
```

137

Kids and Computers

What a long program! If computers are supposed to be time savers, this little beauty misses the boat. The input section is already 470 lines long and we have not even done anything with the data. *Subscripted variables* to the rescue! Like the cavalry, subscripted variables, for that is what this new breed is called, will save the situation. Notice that in order to simplify our variable names in the program above, we used variable names like A2$, A5$, and so on. If we could get the program to invent new variable names, we could clean up this problem. That is exactly what we do. We get the program to add a number to the name of a variable and use that numbered variable for a new memory location. Watch now how we do it: ⇨

```
10 PRINT "ENTER LIST"
20 PRINT "WHEN FINISHED
   ENTER 'END' "
30 LET S = 1
40 INPUT A$(S)
50 IF A$(S) = "END" THEN END
60 LET S = S + 1
70 GOTO 40
```

The first two lines are just our old friends, entry prompts. Line 30 starts a counter variable (called S for subscript) at the value of 1. Line 40 is just an input line, except that the variable to be filled from the keyboard is a strange one. We can see that it is a string variable, for subscripted variables can be used for strings or numbers (but not for both!), depending on whether the suffix character $ is attached. The important part of the variable is the extra variable S in parentheses. This part is the subscript. Notice that the first time through the program the input variable name will be A$(1), because S = 1. Suppose we type in ORANGE JUICE at the prompt. Then line 40 will set A$(1) equal to "ORANGE JUICE." At line 50 the program checks to see if A$(1) equals "END", which it does not. It is still the great O.J. Line 60 adds one to S to make S = 2, and line 70 sends the program back in its loop to line 40. Now, with S equal to 2, a new input variable is waiting for data—A$(2). This variable, invented by the looping program, is filled by typing in COFFEE. The loop continues until at S = 7 we enter END. Now line 50 has its day and the program ends.

Nothing in particular is visible on the computer screen to suggest that the list is anywhere to be found, but inside the RAM are seven variable names, each holding an item on the list. We can prove this by extending the program this way: ⇨

```
50 IF A$(S) = "END" THEN
     GOTO 80
```

This continues the program at line 80 after the word END is entered. Now we add lines: ⇨

```
 80 PRINT "ENTER 'YES'
      TO SEE THE LIST";
 90 INPUT A$
100 IF A$ = "NO" THEN END
110 LET T = 1
120 PRINT A$(T)
130 LET T = T + 1
140 GOTO 120
```

When the prompt appears, and we type anything but NO, the program will print out: ⇨

```
ORANGE JUICE
COFFEE
CORN FLAKES
MILK
CANNED SPINACH
MUSTARD
END

BAD SUBSCRIPT ERROR IN 120
```

The last line is an error message that means that T turned into a number that was no good at line 120. That number on most microcomputers is 10. You cannot use subscripts larger than 10 unless you reserve some memory for the list in advance. This is done by the BASIC command (a function, really) called DIM, which is short for DIMENSION. The DIM command can be used to reserve subscripts up to the limit of RAM memory. You do it (usually) in the first few lines of a program like this: ⇨

```
5 DIM A$(50)
```

which makes sure that subscripted string variables named A$ can have subscripts from 0 to 50, fifty-one different items. To dimension a numeric list the command just drops the $ as   ⇨

```
5 DIM A$(50)
6 DIM B(30)
```

which reserves 51 string variables named A$( ) and 31 numeric variables named B( ). Notice that the variable A$, used to hold the prompted input, and the variable A$( ), the subscripted variables, are not at all the same to the computer and consequently should be seen as different by you also. Finally on this topic, notice that S was used for the subscript to load the list and T for the subscript to read the list. Again, the computer's memory could not care less how the subscript was named, it only referenced the letter A, the $, and the parentheses to identify the list.

Subscripted variables can contain more than a single subscript. When two subscripts are used in the variable name, the variable can store information that would normally be shown in a table and call the values of the variable by reference to the subscripts, that is, by reference to where in the table the item is located. Suppose, for example, we wanted to store all the basic commands and functions that we now know in a single table. Such a table might look like this:

BASIC CODE		
Direct Commands	**Program Commands**	**Functions**
PRINT	PRINT	+
GOTO	GOTO	−
NEW	INPUT	*
RUN	LET	/
LIST	IF ... THEN	↑ or ^
SAVE	DIM	SQR
LOAD	END	(TRIG)
CONT		(LOG)
		RND
		TAB
		(STRING)

The table contains 3 columns and as many as 11 rows. That means we need at most 3 times 11, or 33 variable names. If these names were subscripted by the column number and then by the row number, we could locate any item by its column-row identity.

We start the program by dimensioning the variable BC$ (for BASIC Code) in line 10: ⇨

```
10  DIM BC$(3,11)
```

This line sets up space for 33 variables (actually 48 because the subscripts really start at zero), each of which can be called by a double subscript on the BC$. Next we set up lines to input the table: ⇨

```
20  C=1
30  R=1
40  PRINT "ENTER TABLE
      BY COLUMNS"
50  PRINT "ENTER COLUMN ";C;
      "ROW "; R
60  PRINT "ENTER 'Z' IF NO
      ROW ENTRY"
```

This sets the column subscript at 1, the first column, and the row subscript also at 1. It also sets up the input prompts and tells what to do if there is no datum for a particular variable, such as column 1, row 10. ⇨

```
70   INPUT BC$(C,R)
80   R = R + 1
90   IF R = 12 THEN C = C + 1
100  IF R = 12 AND C = 4 THEN
       GOTO 130
110  IF R = 12 AND C<4 THEN
       R = 1
120  GOTO 50
130  END
```

These lines get and check the input and increment the counter for the column and row subscripts. Notice that the subscripts are pushed up and checked to see if they get out of bounds. When they do, the program ends. Also notice the need to reset the row counter (line 110) whenever the column number changes. I forgot to do this when I first wrote this example, and the program crashed with a BAD SUBSCRIPT ERROR IN LINE 70. The END command at line 130 could just as well have been a new segment of program to print out the table or recover the command name when the column-row numbers were entered. The point here, however, is not to generate a program to do something right now but to show how masses of data can be stored because the machine can automatically make its own variable names.

By this time it must be apparent that computer programming is not a mysterious and difficult task but rather requires the development of certain skills in spotting where the glitches may occur. In a way this ability is like the ability we all have when we get to know anything. In particular, the computer, because of its flexibility, has been likened by some authors to a pet animal that we get to know by playing with it. This idea was part of the motivation for the development of special programming languages for children. The best known of these is the LOGO language. But I want to emphasize that the language itself is not the central aspect of the LOGO principle. Rather, it is programming itself. Learning to program a computer lets you get to know a complicated system outside yourself. This feature of computer programming may account for a large part of our feeling that knowing how to program is more than simply programming. It is not all being able to get the machine to do some particular thing. Indeed, it hardly matters what the program is. The doing of the job constitutes its own reason for being.

Pupils in The Children's Computer School, both kids and adults, can enroll in computer lab sections where they come to the classroom, sit down at a machine, and do anything they want. Very often our teachers note that the child or the adult is not writing particular programs but rather is just fooling around. This usually takes the form of trying out little bits of program code just to see what happens. One case in particular that was interesting and unexpected was that of a 14-year-old girl who just wrote this fragment of program code and ran it: ⇨

```
10 C = 10
20 C = 2 * C
30 PRINT C
40 GOTO 20
```

The program began to print out numbers, lots and lots of numbers. Shortly numbers of a new kind began to appear. Finally the program quit with the number that looked like this: ⇨

```
5.3 . . . E+37
```

What a strange number! It turns out that our student had gotten past the point where our computers could print the number in standard notation, and the computer had switched, as they all do, to exponential notation. The number above is merely

$$5.3 \times 10 \uparrow 37$$

a very big number. She had discovered exponential notation. Because she was a student at our school she could get her instructor to explain it all very quickly. But even while writing and revising programs by yourself, unexpected results often lead to new insights that can also be tested by further exploration. These discoveries can be exploited by teachers and other sources of instruction and information to expand your computer horizons.

Before we continue it will be of some interest, although of no current practical value, to know that the programs we wrote here were accomplished with a very small subcollection of BASIC commands. The interesting fact is that these commands are a sufficient collection in principle to let you write any program that can be entered in a microcomputer in BASIC. However, any microcomputer you buy will contain a much richer collection of BASIC than was used here. This will make things

Kids and Computers

like loops within loops, as in our double-subscript program, so easy that the intricacies of the code we used here will seem childish. The newer BASIC operating systems give so much flexibility in writing programs that your program skills will be multiplied by the power of the language.

The looping command that you will probably use most often in BASIC programming is the FOR ... NEXT command. Just like IF ... THEN, the FOR ... NEXT command is composed of two and sometimes three code words. The important feature of the command is that if a loop must be completed a known number of times, that information can be embedded in the command and thus save the need for a loop counter. Instead of the loop counter variable, for example, $C = C + 1$, the FOR ... NEXT command uses an *index variable*. To give you the flavor of such FOR ... NEXT loops, we will rewrite lines 70 to 130 of our program for the BASIC CODE TABLE side by side with the original program lines.

```
 70 INPUT BC$(C,R)              70 FOR C = 1 TO 3
 80 R = R + 1                   80 FOR R = 1 TO 12
 90 IF R = 12 THEN C = C + 1    90 INPUT BC$(C,R)
100 IF R = 12 AND C = 4 THEN   100 NEXT R
    GOTO 130                   110 NEXT C
110 IF R = 12 AND C<4 THEN
    R = 1
120 GOTO 50
130 END
```

Notice that the FOR part of the command is really a loop counter with a starting and finishing value. The NEXT command is an automatic "plus 1" adder, which also contains its own GOTO command. The FOR ... NEXT command is, as you see, simply a way to simplify program coding; it adds to the intrinsic power of program code to solve programming problems.

This is also true of the command GOSUB . . . RETURN, which is a way to branch to another part of the program, just like a GOTO, but with the feature that the RETURN command takes you back to the line after the particular GOSUB that sent the program to the new location. This could all be done with GOTOs but would take more remembering on your part, especially if the subroutine was called several times from different places in the program. To handle that job with GOTOs would require conditionals at the subroutine to determine where the program was to go back to on each pass.

Finally, the code READ . . . DATA is a useful BASIC command that lets the program fill variables (usually subscripted) from inside the program itself. This command works by assigning program lines to what are called DATA statements. An example is   ⇨

```
10 DATA JOHN SMITH,
   JANE BROWN,JIM DOE
```

These may be the names of students in a school class. In some dialects of BASIC this command requires that no spaces be allowed in the DATA line, except those that are part of the actual data. Observe also that a delimiter—the comma—is used after each datum. In order to load the variables with the data, we need a loop that READs the DATA line. This READ command can be anywhere in the program, since READ sends the program to the first DATA line in the program.   ⇨

```
20 FOR N = 1 TO 3
30 READ N$
40 PRINT N$
50 NEXT N
60 END
```

This program would print out the three names in the data statement because each time through the loop the READ command would read a DATA item, and then it would be printed in line 40.

These three additional commands are described not because I am intent on presenting a complete list, for I am not.

145

Kids and Computers

Rather you should have a sense of the extent over which BASIC commands can range, so that when your child says, "I think I'll READ that DATA statement in a FOR . . . NEXT loop . . . before I call the subroutine," you will know what it is all about. There are many more commands in most BASICs that are included in modern microcomputers. As I have commented before, sometimes the particular command will have a different form from one dialect to another, but the commands we have reviewed here are common to all BASIC dialects. We have not included the variations, even though they are important to learn when you finally settle on your own machine. For example, the command to clear the screen given inside a BASIC program is CLEAR for the HP-85, CLS for the Radio Shack TRS-80, PRINT" ♥ " for the Commodore PET®, and HOME for the Apple II.

BASIC is only one of perhaps 25 different programming languages in more or less common use. At the entry level, there are only a few languages suitable for use in learning to program. In the opinion of a large and vocal minority of programming instructors, BASIC does not qualify as a really good programming language because it does not foster structured programming. To grasp the flavor of this criticism, you must understand that these instructors want more thinking before you sit down at the machine. Their notion is that "efficiency" is improved by preplanning the form of the program. Such preplanning can be done using BASIC just as well as it can using a structured language like Pascal. But the critics' point is that the language does not force you to plan in advance, which a language like Pascal does.

A common planning technique often used by BASIC programmers to develop the program structure before getting to the computer is called *flowcharting.* This method of planning involves drawing a diagram that shows the parts of the program and what decisions and actions have to be taken to accomplish the program purpose. Consider the following example: Suppose we want to write a program to search for a particular last name in a list of names that is stored in a subscripted variable. Before we begin at the machine, we could outline the problem by drawing a chart or graph that shows the logical flow of the program. Figure 32 shows such a flowchart.

Since BASIC is so highly interactive that it points out your mistakes to you as you make them, systematic planning is rarely needed. BASIC lets you write programs the way that Mozart wrote music, by improvising as you go along. Of course this is not the most efficient or systematic way to get the work done, and indeed, if you were writing programs as a profession you would want to use a structured language. But for fun and for programs whose innards you understand, BASIC is hard to beat. I have heard it argued, and I agree with the sentiment, that unless you are writing programs with more than a thousand lines of code, BASIC is probably as efficient as any other programming language.

Although the notion of a structured language has many aspects, one central idea concerns its ability to handle complicated conditionals. For example, suppose that the form of the program logic we want to execute is the following: If condition X is true, we want the machine to do a certain procedure, say Y. However, if condition X is false, we want another procedure, say Z, to be performed. Some forms of BASIC solve this problem by using a special form of IF ... THEN, whose

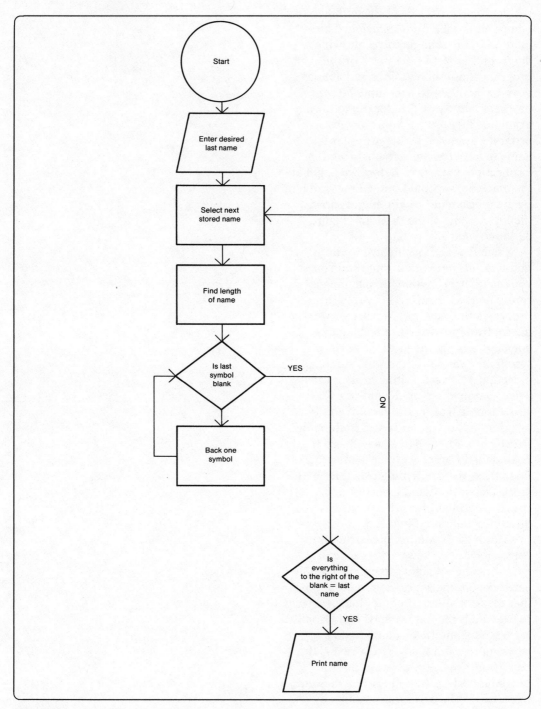

Figure 32: A flow chart for a computer program.

syntax is IF . . . THEN . . . ELSE, where a new procedure can follow the ELSE command if the IF part is false. This solves the problem if procedures Y and Z are only a simple action, say printing one message or another. But if Y requires five lines of code and Z requires eight lines, the IF . . . THEN . . . ELSE does not solve our problem. We would be forced to solve the problem in this fashion: ⇨

```
100 IF X THEN 200
110 [start procedure Z]
        •
        •
180 [end procedure Z]
190 GOTO 250
200 [start procedure Y]
        •
240 [end procedure Y]
250 [continue with the rest
    of the program]
```

This is not too bad, but consider the form of program we would need for some double branching through conditional statements such as: ⇨

```
100 IF NOT A THEN 160
110 IF B THEN 140
120 [do procedure P2]
130 GOTO 200
140 [do procedure P1]
150 GOTO 200
160 IF C THEN 170
170 [do procedure P4]
180 GOTO 200
190 [do procedure P3]
200 [continue the program]
```

Before you say, "Well, it's not too bad," remember that lines 120, 140, 170, and 190 may each be several lines long. Trying to keep track of what is going on in this tail-chasing set of IF . . . THENs might convert anyone to a structured programming language. The point is that a structured language would permit these complex branches to be coded without the skipping around with GOTO statements that BASIC requires. But the telling point for BASIC is that people do write programs with this kind of tail-chasing, and in fact the programmers seem to enjoy untangling a logical structure as formidable as this. When I was teaching an advanced game-programming course, I had students come up to show me how convoluted their programs had become. They were proud of their ability to track the flow of logic that the complexities imposed.

Kids and Computers

There is no need to defend BASIC as a programming language for beginners. It is, after all, built into every home microcomputer on the market today. But you should remember that other programming languages do exist and that they were invented because there is no universal solvent for the problems of logic that programs must solve.

Whereas professional programmers fault BASIC as too flimsy to use for serious programming, educators have expressed the thought that BASIC may be too structured for children. A language of interest for such educationally oriented computerists is LOGO. This language is a marvelous high-level interpretive operating system that permits a child to use simple commands to move a screen cursor that draws high-quality figures on the screen—in color. The aim of the developers of the language is that it will teach children geometric concepts that are intrinsic to the constraints the commands impose. In order to draw a square, for example, the child issues the command FORWARD 15, which tells the machine to advance the cursor 15 units and leave a trail. Then the command RIGHT 90 results in a rotation by 90 degrees, which if followed by a new FORWARD 15 and RIGHT 90, etc., will result in a square on the screen. Loops are programmed by the REPEAT command, so the square could be drawn by some syntax such as REPEAT 4 [FORWARD 15 RIGHT 90], which would make the four commands occur by this single line of code.

Notice the interesting fact that the developers of this language have established: that a closed figure must rotate a trace point through 360 units. Now it is all well and good to talk about creativity in children, but any child will be hard pressed to comprehend the strange unit—the degree—as a plausible representation of space. In addition, the apparent simplicity of the geometric intuitions depends on the child's ability to comprehend the screen as a plane surface facing him or her. Some children get the left-right screaming meemies out of this confusion. But the main point is this, I think: LOGO attempts to replace the instrinsically serial linguistic syntax of the computer with a geometric logic. Insofar as the machine can simulate such geometries, program code that implements these ideas can be written. Just why it is educationally advantageous for children to program shape and form instead of time and structure is not at all clear and obvious. Indeed, the development of these geometric intuitions seems to be achieved quite well by all normal children. The need is to help kids grasp the temporal logic of sequential decisions. This is what most computer programs require, and it is the intellectual heart of learning how to program.

A nice way to tie up these issues might be to construe programming languages as a developmental process in children and adults. Perhaps very young children should start their machine skill development by using a geometric programming language like LOGO. They might then graduate to a more serial language such as BASIC. After mastering the logic of BASIC programming, they could explore the world of structured programming with perhaps Pascal, and finally trace back to the roots of the system through machine-language programming.

Have you been impatient for the next COMPUQUIZ? Well, here it is at last!

COMPUQUIZ #3

1. How would your computer evaluate 4 * 12/3 + 3 ?

2. To find the length of a string variable you would use the string function _____.

3. One thing a microcomputer is good at is doing the same thing over and over again. One way to do this is with a counter variable. What is a counter variable?

4. In an IF . . . THEN statement if the IF clause were false, where would the program go next?

5. What is a subscripted variable? Can it be a string variable?

6. When do you use the DIM command?

7. What is a double subscript? What can you use it for?

You have reached a high point in your knowledge of BASIC programming. If the material in this chapter seemed fairly complicated, you are on the right track. It *was* quite complicated. But if you read through it again you will find that it begins to come together. You and your children can quiz each other on the BASIC code you have learned, and by the time you are ready to sit down at your microcomputer, it should all become quite clear. The main problem will be that you will have no one to ask if you get stuck. Remember this: You cannot hurt the computer by anything you enter from the keyboard. As the machine accuses you of making error after syntax error, you will finally hit on the correct coding of the program line, and lo and behold, it will all clear up. Don't falter; it really is easy! The computer keeps confusing you because it cannot accept approximations to what you want to do. You must state your commands exactly.

Chapter 10

Looking Ahead

A child who can program has two strings to the bow. First and most obvious, he or she is at home with a computer. Second, and less obvious, is a flexibility of thought that we believe the programming skill can produce. One of our very young programming students was having some difficulty figuring out how to clock the speed of a computer generating an answer to an arithmetic problem. Some computers have clocks in them that can be accessed by a reserved string variable name. The ones we were using in school were of this kind, but the child's teacher had not yet revealed this special feature of the machine. As a result, the child worked out a system for getting input on each cycle of a loop, and when the correct input occurred, he checked the loop counter to see how many cycles (i.e., how long) it had taken. An idea like this comes only with opportunities to use systems that can expose a repetitive operation that is easily counted. Once such an idea takes form, as it did for this child, he equips himself with a new general skill. When insights of this kind have occurred in historical contexts, as, for example, to Galileo watching the swinging lamps in the church at Pisa, they are thought to constitute profound intellectual breakthroughs. When children accomplish similar feats in front of a computer, their achievements must be recognized for what they are: deep insights into the logical structure of the world.

In his interesting and exciting book, *The Mighty Micro,* the late Christopher Evans foresaw the development of curricular material for small computers that would, or at least could, replace the entire public school system. He anticipated that in the mid 1980s microcomputers would be available that were effectively programmed with school material and that would be able to teach this material to children using both speech and text. He based these projections on the local success of synthetic speech devices such as Texas Instruments' Speak & Spell and on what he had heard about teaching machines and programmed instruction. The Speak & Spell is a beautiful little device that speaks a word from a spelling list stored in its memory. The child then types in from the alphabetical keyboard (not a qwerty!) the letters that are needed to correctly spell the word. If the child is right, the machine praises him or her and goes to the next word. If the child is wrong, he or she gets two more tries and then is shown the correct spelling. At the end of each session the child gets a score and is encouraged to try again or to proceed to harder lists.

Kids and Computers

The machine uses a ROM-based word list that can be replaced (with some effort) by other program materials. Complete with its keyboard, screen, speaker, and microcomputer, the machine sells for less than $75. When you compare the enormous technical achievement the machine represents to its modest cost, you can easily be carried away by visions of literacy spreading throughout the world, borne by this TI teacher. Unhappily, I do not believe it will happen, nor do I believe it could. The intrinsic merit of the machine is its impressive technology. Parents (including me) are overwhelmed by the incredible capabilities of something so small and so cheap. But a child, who knows nothing of this technical tour de force, finds that working at the spelling machine may be as intrinsically boring as a classroom or a workbook session. Insofar as parents buy these things, they will continue to be sold based on the hope that somehow the computer will turn drudgery to joy. Nothing could be further from the truth.

Attempts to scan the future seem to me doomed to dismal defeat. However, many changes that occur in the larger community occur first in smaller assemblies. A conscientious reading of specialty magazines, trade journals, and corporate reports can often tell us with some confidence where the commercial world is putting its money. The lead time between such commercial investments and the public availability of a product or service is fairly long, so that we can anticipate what may be on the horizon in the computer world regarding family use of computers for entertainment and education, as well as the implications of the computers' impact on the intellectual life of our children. As I remarked in 1959 in a book I edited entitled *Automatic Teaching: the*

State of the Art,

The development of a successful machine that will teach a person the complex of interlocking symbolic and verbal knowledge that is the mark of an education is equivalent to a general theory of learning and teaching.

I then went on to indicate that such a theory did not then exist, nor did I see how it could be developed without the detailed study of how children (and adults) learn, and what they need, environmentally and internally, in order to learn. Other contributors to that book tried to make inroads in those areas. But none of them believed, as Christopher Evans apparently did twenty years later, that an improvement in the machinery will solve these deep scientific problems. Until we know more about the nature of human learning, we must still make use of the same technologies and concepts that were available to Aristotle.

In this context it may be of interest to hear something about the value of computer programs that are made to teach people how to program. Among the hundreds of adult students at The Children's Computer School, there are some, perhaps eight or nine, who arrived after having bought a computer that came complete with a programmed course in BASIC. Many of them were confused and frustrated in their attempts to master what then seemed an impossible skill. One of my teachers remarked that she was afraid that one particular student had been so put off by the program for learning BASIC that came with his machine that he planned to sell the machine and give up the whole enterprise. She persuaded him to hang on for the first four hours. Then, it became love at second sight. He was, after all, very interested in computers—he had bought one.

154

This need to be taught by a human teacher seems to be thoroughly documented in the history of education. Even learning how to use a computer, which some think may supplant teachers, requires the same personal touch and understanding of the pitfalls and confusions that are often unique to each person. What a good teacher does is to recognize areas of difficulty and employ the appropriate teaching strategy to get the student over the hurdles of strangeness and fear of the unknown that are part of every adventure in learning.

As a consequence of these considerations, I see no immediate prospect for some revolutionary change in childhood education. I do, however, see the need for children today to learn more and different things than they did when I went to school. At first glance what they need to learn seems clear and obvious—add more science, more math, more foreign language, more social science, more technology (including, perhaps, computer literacy), more writing skills, and so on. But stop! How is all this possible? The time available is the same, and my days were as filled as my children's. I believe the answer is as it has always been: to shortchange on some items in order to allow room for others. As I recall them, the shortchanged items in my day were usually vocational. The principle was that they would not be missed if they were no longer relevant. For example, I spent many hours in high school learning drafting skills. Today, draftsmen who know how to letter neatly are on the way out since computerized drafting machines (CADs, short for computer-aided design) have taken over much of this job. I still know how to design a cam, but what's the need? Such mechanical control systems, as, for example, those used in automotive distributors, have been replaced by microchips at one-fiftieth the cost of a cam and

follower, and as a side benefit they make the ignition system 100 times more reliable.

There is no way to know at the time whether a mistake is being made when any particular subject is deleted from the curriculum. For example, Latin fell by the wayside when psychologists pronounced the doctrine of "mental exercise" faulty. The fact that this may have been a bad way to sell the need for Latin in the first place is probably the culprit. Learning Latin may be good for the soul, whether it is good for English grammar or not. Indeed, how do we know that English grammar is so valuable? The answer is that some aspects of the curriculum contain within themselves the seeds of mental flora. I am not certain that I can identify them all, but some are primary and most of us agree about them. My concern about the future of your child is that there is a new star in the constellation of fundamental knowledge. That supernova in the educational firmament is the ability to write computer programs. The importance of computers does not, I think, as Christopher Evans believes, lie in their uses. Rather, their value lies simply in their existence. Like Latin, if computers are only valuable for what they can teach us about math or spelling, then like Latin they must surely drop away from the curriculum. But the study of computers would be bound to return just as the study of Latin has never really left, because computer literacy is also good for the soul.

The ability to program a computer is a skill that is central to the intelligent comprehension of today's world. Whether the expanded use of computers is in home multipurpose machines (as it surely will be for the next few years) or computers are deftly incorporated into existing special-purpose machines, i.e., household appliances, to make these machines "smart," contact with computers will increase rapidly. Regardless of whether computers will or will not shortly be programmed to teach Hindi and calculus, or whether new machines will fit in your pocket to display, recite, and historically interpret the preamble to the Constitution, computer programming as an intellectual exercise is a must. In my view this is because computer programs make possible a new form of analysis and synthesis that is separate and distinct from linguistic or mathematical knowledge or methods. Books and pen and paper are the technical support system for language and mathematics. The third addition to the two primary ways of understanding our world and ourselves is computer programming. Computers as machines represent the technical adjunct to this form of understanding. They are the support system for this new way of knowing and thinking. The idea that pen and paper seem more "natural" than a computer chip and its accessories would be lost instantly on a marvelling cave man who was shown even our most modest writing and drawing technology.

This position is taken and supported by others in the computer literacy field. Sometimes, however, these scientists lose sight of the general principle that is involved, and then they tend to concentrate on the advantages they perceive in some specific programming language. The LOGO language is a consequence and an example of this belief. The idea is that some programming languages serve better to acquaint children with computers than others do. So far as I can find, there is no evidence that this is true. Indeed, children who learn BASIC or Pascal as their first programming language usually come to the same class of insights and a similar understanding of computers. Now it is often the case that the Pascal child will spend more time planning before

writing, while the BASIC child will spend more time exploring and testing. But even if I were convinced of the validity of these observations, I certainly would not want to bet on which approach produces a wiser adult. Indeed our position at The Children's Computer School is that regardless of the language, it is learning how to program that is the heart of the matter.

Knowing how to program really means knowing the parts of some intellectual task. It also means that you and your child know how things are connected to each other in terms of their temporal logic. This skill demands that we use our temporal "eye." This metaphoric eye is the name I give to the basis for our perception of time. It lets us look into the past through our memories and into the future through our imagination. This symmetry of memory and imagination and its unfolding at "now" is what a given point in the development of a program represents. In a way, what the computer does is force us to recognize this symmetry of memory and imagination as the single continuum that it is. In this way our visual-eye-based geometrical sense is augmented by that central-eye-based temporal sense. The programming effort exploits this ability and sharpens our perception of coherent temporal structures.

The child of tomorrow should, as a consequence of his or her acquaintance with computation in its general sense, be better able to scan and foresee the consequences of personal action and decision. This foresight depends, in our terms, on the present integration of past information relative to the current moment. These aspects of the past that are important to the here and now may not be simply and directly connected to the present and the future. Our knowledge and actions of the past may require conditional branches and distant GOTO jumps in order to become part of the present and the future. We hardly have a discipline in our schools today that attends to these skills that Alfred Korzybski and S.I. Hayakawa called *time binding.* Yet it is an important ability— common to features of the social, the physical, and the psychic world.

Some analysts and prognosticators say that the speed with which computers are developing may lead us past this current state where programming skills are needed. New machines that reprogram themselves to solve idiosyncratic aspects of our needs will make it unnecessary to know how to program. Other machines will become so dedicated to specific problems that they will no longer be thought of as reprogrammable. As an example of such beliefs, consider the experience of one of our beginning students. He was so keen to get along with learning to program that he signed up for 10 hours of laboratory classes at the school. Because our classroom space is limited, we like to check to see if the student can use a rental computer at home. We subsequently discovered that the mother, who had a small home-office business, had a microcomputer at home to address her mailing labels. Since it had been sold to her for this special purpose, complete with proprietary software, neither she nor her child realized that it was a useful and eminently usable general-purpose computer. He does his practice at home now. But the point is that such single-purpose machines could be made and might better serve their intended purpose if they were not reprogrammable.

Computers for a single special purpose are now and will continue to be built into various machines to exercise their special brand of intelligent control. Household appliances will be routinely fitted with a computer to monitor and control their

operations. Since the intricate tracery of local impurities that lend these chips of silicon their power to command minute electric currents is so cheap to mass produce, it is hard not to believe that the future lies in machines for special tasks. Some consolidation of functions may occur. For example, the small-business cash register may also be connected by a modem to the credit-card computer for checking and debiting your account. At the end of the day the cash register may tally receipts, generate inventory-control data, and place orders to suppliers to restock the shelves. But there is bound to be a continuation of multipurpose machines that will adapt to new programs that can be installed in them from off-line mass storage. These machines will be user programmable and may serve primarily to teach programming. This skill may not be necessary as a practical pursuit or even to develop games and educational material, for those programs may all be available in cheap special-purpose devices. But the ability to program should be seen as an adjunct to a child's education. When viewed in this light, there is no future that can diminish its importance.

But what exactly will the future demand from those of us who will work and play with microcomputers? There are two important components of the technical world that will surely interact with our home microcomputers. These systems are the telephone network and television. The United States telephone switching system allows almost any individual location in the country to be connected to other specific geographical points. This will allow easy interlinks between and among individual computers and their owners. The result of this transition from simple two-way voice communication to the ability of individuals to transmit data from computer to computer will make new social and political structures possible and probably inevitable.

The other major communication channel—television—which unlike the telephone diffuses information from a central point, will also become interactive with the coming generations of home computers that are connected to them. You will be able to interact with educational and other program material because the video signal will also contain information that your computer can read and use. I do not think it is likely that methods to talk back to network headquarters will expand much from their current experimental forms, as in the QUBE system. Such response systems demand transmission facilities in the home. Whereas the telephone provides such service by using very inexpensive transmitting equipment, the nature of television places a greater economic demand on the system.

The connection of a microcomputer in your home to a telephone line by a modem lets you connect to an enormous warehouse of programs and data. As we said in Chapter 4, this connection may be the most important peripheral in your system. Because a central computer to which your machine is connected can store inexhaustible quantities of information, the need to buy or write programs to do specific jobs may vanish. Even today you can call up *The New York Times* on your computer and print out just those stories you want to read after scanning the whole paper on your video screen. The same concept can be applied to any (or all) books, periodicals, or data bases such as stock market reports. A capability of this kind certainly limits any real need to know how to write a computer program.

Yet the point made earlier, that the central importance of the computer is found in programming it, is still a valid one. Although it is unlikely that you would want to write a program or suite of programs to do word processing, you might want to write a simple, personal program for your machine. But even this may not be an adequate motive to justify learning to program. It must be the case that these excuses for learning to program are just that. One important value, of course, is that knowing how to program leads to a deeper understanding of the machine itself. Computers are all around us and will continue to increase in number. If you do not know what they can do, you are missing out on knowing about an important product of modern scientific thought. But once again, this justification may only be of quaint historical interest. My view of the real need to program is to give you a command over the nature of time in the organization of thought. The center of my argument is that knowing how to program a computer improves your ability to think. The trouble with this line is that it has been said before about lots of materials—Latin among them. Does such an idea make any sense? Can a child learn to think better?

Many of the intellectual discussions surrounding computers today turn not on whether they can help you to think or to think better but on the question of whether the computer itself can think. This is the image of the giant brain. Does there reside within that maze of circuits a thinking mind? I believe this to be an intrinsically pointless question. We can always define or redefine thinking so that any particular computer can or cannot think. Indeed, what difference could it possibly make if they can or can't? The best opinion in the science of psychology is that the concept of thought is so poorly defined as to be unusable in serious research. Computers certainly calculate better than I do and occasionally play chess better. There are those who would hold then that the computer can think. Good for them. On the other hand, I doubt that it could do my job. But the day it can take my work away from me is the day that I will reevaluate my position.

The ability of computers to do some things better than a person is like the ability of a steam shovel to move more earth than a man. Obviously, we invent devices to reduce the effort we expend in work, but we do not want our own work to vanish. How can we possibly defend this position? There is no way in principle to protect our own intrinsic value as human beings if our work, or whatever else we do, is all that we represent. Machines will certainly replace us in most if not all the things we now do. What then is our intrinsic purpose? The answer to that question when stripped of its mystical overtones must be that we should lead a full and good life. Some of that endeavor, if not the major part of it, must depend on our mental activity. To some extent we design and define the universe we live in. To that end, the effective use of our minds is part of our biological and spiritual heritage. To expand that function is to enhance our lives.

Thinking better must be the one effort that should serve to occupy our lives. Ways to improve our lot always have and always will depend on the use of our minds. Whatever accomplishes this enhancement to our thinking gives humankind an added edge on survival. If anything will protect us from self-destruction in one form or another, it will be the power of thought to move the world. Such thinking may take many forms. Indeed, it may lead us to new spiritual adventures as well as material advances. But in the final analysis we need to hone our minds to a sharp edge and to use that tool to rededicate ourselves and

our children. The puny measures we have used with such success in the past surely show that faith in our mental powers can move mountains. Perhaps the new skills demanded by this new artifact, the microcomputer, can augment our arsenal. The historical record demonstrates that our intellectual efforts have always added to our material well-being. Perhaps some new improvements in our modes of thought can do as much for our social existence. This leads us to another important question: Can the computer alter a child's personality?

A parent of one our pupils came to me after her daughter's second lesson at the computer school. She was worried about what this course of study would do to her child. Marian had always been a neat and well-organized child, and her mother was worried that learning to program a computer would increase this tendency toward overorganization. "I'm worried," she said, "that Marian will become a compulsive and hypertense person. She works so hard to get everything just right. Don't you think working on the computer will emphasize these traits and make her worse off?" This is a natural fear. It reflects the view that certain kinds of intellectual activities influence the nature of one's emotional and affective life-style. Before we examine this issue, let us consider the expectations of Brian's father. Brian was one of our more "laid back" students. His father had enrolled him at the school with first the secret, then the strongly stated, hope that Brian would become more focused and precise in his day-to-day behavior. "Shouldn't computing help my son get straightened out?" he asked. We could not see clearly where Brian needed straightening out, but his father's hope obviously reflected the same principle as Marian's mother's fear. Could we answer either parent's concern from the basis of our experience, or was there any scientific evidence that would be used to reassure these anxious parents?

You must accept first the primary truth that learning to program, or learning anything else for that matter, is not going to change a child's personality. If it could do this, we would have in our hands a discovery beyond anything that Freud or any other psychologist could ever have imagined. We have seen children go through our curriculum with all kinds of attitudes, interests, and talents. The overwhelming majority have been successful in learning to write microcomputer programs. If any other changes occurred in their nature or general demeanor, it was not at all obvious to any of their instructors. I think that knowing how to program lets a child release his or her own capacities for the special logical thought that this skill demands. Sometimes this developing skill runs hand-in-hand with other maturing features of the child's growth. In that case the skill may shape the content of the youngster's personality, but I cannot believe that this skill will change the structure of that personality.

There is no reason to fear that learning how to use a computer will convert your child into an unthinking robot. Indeed, the chances are better that the child's thought processes will be expanded and enhanced. As we have seen before, the child who knows how to program learns how to simulate temporal processes, how to analyze logical flow patterns, how to divide a problem into subparts, and how to weld his imagination to his memory to form an unbroken continuum from past to future. In Chapter 3, I remarked on the cognitive safety of learning to use a computer; there is no reason at the end of this journey to revise that statement.

Chapter 11
Evaluating Computer Education

We have spiraled up through the micro-computer world, touching at various turns on the purposes, designs, structures, languages, and values of microcomputers for you and your children. This spiral motif was meant to ensure that the many points of our discussion were reviewed and amplified as we turned and reversed through the computer world. Now we are home—and at home—with this new technology, and it is time for a broad look back to see the implications of what we have traversed.

Structures first; the world of microcomputers is here and in a form that will probably stabilize over the next few years. There are two aspects of the microcomputer to impact on us at home. First the CPUs and small ROMs will find their way into many, if not most, of our household systems and devices. Such things as dishwashers, refrigerators, lawn mowers, power hand tools, heating and cooling systems, intrusion alarms, telephones, TVs, hi-fi systems, and many other devices will be controlled by special-purpose microcomputers. These enhancements will not serve to reduce the cost of these devices; rather their reliability, and probably their long-term serviceability will be improved.

The second aspect of the introduction of microcomputers into the home will be in the form of either special-purpose (e.g., word processors) or general-purpose computers that can be used by us for a multitude of tasks. The properties of the computer that make this multi-tasking possible are, as we have seen, the programmability of the machine, its enormous speed of operation, and its large and essentially infallible memory. These features of computers will be exploited in many areas, but especially in their role as educational aids for children; as entertainment devices for playing games and developing other skills; as memory banks for files, lists, and other memoranda that need to be remembered, reorganized, and recalled in special ways; and as machines to manage numbers, in such areas as figuring budgets, taxes, expenses, and so on.

The same features that make the machines useful at home will also make them useful in the work place, including private businesses and professions. All the advantages that large corporations found when they adopted multimillion dollar computers will be available to every business and profession at one-thousandth the cost or less. And of course the ability of the microcomputer to "talk" to other machines, either at work or for work, will extend enormously the value of the machine in the home. There are some who believe that the return of the home-based worker is imminent. Whether this is true for large numbers of people or not may be debatable; certainly many of us and especially our children, will find it possible and feasible to work at home because of the computer.

One primary consequence of the widespread use of the microchip in business will be to replace paper as the repository of information. Not only is silicon cheaper than paper pulp or even plastic paper feed stocks, but it is enormously smaller in bulk. The increasing storage capacity of the current crop of ROM chips may also be supplemented by *bubble* memories and other exotic storage systems. The main advantage of such storage, however, is the ease of retrieval of the information in them. When information is stored in this elegant form, it can be recovered extremely quickly and reorganized even faster. The kinds of unforeseen consequences of events of this kind may even include the regrowth of our large stands of forests.

When a society finds itself using more and more people to transform and increase information rather than material goods, then a machine that advances that kind of activity is clearly the machine of the future. The value of the computer in particular is further extended by its ability to command and control other machines and systems. The most prominent of these applications is the industrial robot. Here, the benefit of the computer's information processing feats, when it is buried in another machine, combines and extends the complexity of work that the mechanical arm can perform. The limits of such robotization of the blue-collar work place remains to be seen. The factory of the near future is bound to consist not merely of rigid assembly lines operated by humans who serve to control and modulate the stamped-out products. It will also boast freely moving, or perhaps even freely roaming, robots that can exert enormous strength with great precision. Indeed, the factory becomes the robot. Products then may be tailored more exactly to their purpose, and "handmade," the true meaning of "manufacture," will once again appear in the marketplace.

Overconcern for the displacement of workers in our factories by these intelligent robots is probably misdirected, even though unemployment is a personal and national tragedy. Although some estimates of such job losses are higher, a good guess is that only 1% of the work force will be directly affected in any given year. The current number of employees in durable-goods industries is estimated by the Bureau of Labor Statistics at 13 million. Of this group perhaps 25% work, say 4 million for the sake of argument, at assembly-line jobs on tasks that could be handled by an intelligent robot. This is probably a high estimate, but let us examine the consequences. Industry experience indicates that a robot can probably replace four workers, with the cost of the robot about equal to their combined yearly pay. This is because the capital cost for robots will not get very cheap. The robots' computer "heart" is only a small and inexpensive part; their mechanical and electrical components will keep their cost near $100,000 a copy. Therefore, to replace all the possible workers would cost just under $100 billion, quite a bit more than all of American industry spends on all its capital investment each year. The result is that the replacements will take place over time and, consequently, can be accommodated by normal attrition through retirement and job transfers. If robot production is to replace all appropriate workers in, say 10 years, we will have to invest $10 billion per year on robots alone. This is probably high by a factor of 10, and consequently we can expect force reductions of perhaps

32,000 to 40,000 per year attributable to robots. With a work force of say 40 million, the reduction amounts to about 1%.

A real concern will be the loss of white-collar information processing jobs. Here the numbers are much more telling. Within the private sector we may expect a reduction in the lowest-level clerical and filing ranks of up to one-half by the 1990s. This work force amounts to about 15 million. The machines that will replace these workers are cheap, unlike their factory cousins. The government bureaucracies will probably fare better because they can generate new tasks for themselves. However, in some segments of public employment such as the postal system, the reductions in manpower made possible by the computer as it is used in new ways for new purposes may be extensive. The primary effect on the work force will be a new selectivity. New jobs will require new skills. These skills will depend on new forms of literacy. We will know these skills as computer literacy.

After my experiences with my three daughters, who all learned to program at home, it became clear that more formalized education was required. By 1979 my wife and I believed we knew how to teach computer skills to children starting at the age of my youngest daughter, Michelle, who learned the ins and outs by age 7. My notes and outlines were taking form as a structured instructional protocol. The central theoretical concept that guided this effort was that classical forms of spacial-geometric-pictorial thinking and logic must be augmented, and occasionally replaced, by temporal-imaginative-memorial logic. The child must learn to substitute an inner temporal eye for the outer spacial eye. Even when you are writing a program to generate graphics or pictures on the computer's screen, the organization of the display must be restructured in your mind's eye into a time-based image. To teach this skill to a child becomes a challenge and a responsibility.

But not all the thought and effort were of such cosmic proportions. Many of the details were mundane. We worked for seven months on the question of the size of the units we should break the subject matter into. All these items were finally decided, often by guess informed by hope, but always with the knowledge that experience would serve us in the end. By the spring of 1980 we started to recruit and train some of our young college and graduate school students in the methods developed so far. Many of them contributed important and ingenious variations and improvements on our original work. In January of 1981 we opened the doors of the first Children's Computer School in New York.

Although we are convinced that to learn to program in BASIC requires certain equipment and student/teacher ratios, there are many books and magazines that can whet your appetite and interest. Some of the more popular computer magazines, such as *Byte* and *Micro*, are aimed at the well-informed hobbyist. Others, such as *Compute, Popular Computing,* and *Personal Computing,* have articles that the beginner can use to improve or develop his program-writing skills. Many books on learning to program in BASIC have been written. I list several of my favorites in the References (see page 181). You may dip into them and discover, as most of us have, that the skill necessary to program does not come from the printed word. The same sentiment goes, of course, for Chapters 5, 7, and 9. The point of those chapters was obviously not to teach you to write programs but rather to acquaint you with the nature and structure of program writing.

Kids and Computers

Our experience leads us to the opinion that you can best learn to program by going to a computer school or by attending a computer course in your child's own school. The problem with the latter is that the educational establishment is neither clear nor comprehensive in its dealings with computers. The primary result of this lack of intimate knowledge of computers and computing is that most schools either assign a science or math teacher to "computers," then buy a computer or two, and finally announce to students and parents that they have a computer program. Nothing could be further from the mark. The computer programs in most schools have several faults. If you know what they are, you will be a better prepared consumer of computer education.

First and foremost is the notion that computers are for general education, that is, they are an "audio-visual" aid for learning the classic subject matter. The teaching-machine image has convinced many school supervisors that computers are a training aid for math, spelling, and other subjects that use flash cards for their comprehension. This is fortified by the appearance of whole suites of programs with names like "Fundamental Phonics and Word Study." These programs are marketed by well-known educational publishers with excellent reputations for textbook material. But a review of these programs by my colleague at Teachers College, Columbia University, Dr. Mary Alice White, suggests that 80% of these "teaching" programs are worthless, and another 19% are only marginally useful. Dr. White and I both agree that perhaps 1% of the program materials available for use as learning aids may be of some value.

Some school computer programs have reached a second stage of recognizing that computers in the schools are for teaching "computer literacy." But this concept, which I have tried to clarify in this book, is used by the schools to cover a multitude of sins. Mostly it is promulgated by a teacher who knows about and likes computers and computing. Through his or her efforts the principal has finally agreed to buy three computers, which are then installed in a science lab, or sometimes a janitor's closet. The kids in the school are all excited by the prospect of studying computers. They quickly find that it's a drag—either they are forced to learn how to write programs to solve math or science problems, or else the three most active and aggressive kids in the class take over the machines, and it's sit and watch time for the rest of the class. The teacher is rewarded by keeping these "hackers" on the machines, for they learn every exotic trick in the programmer's book. This makes the teacher feel that something useful is happening. Your child and my child may learn something by watching over a shoulder, but that is the extent of their contact with the computer.

Some of our best schools and most progressive school systems display these faults. The reasons are fairly obvious. Knowing how to program and use a computer is not the same as knowing how to teach these skills to youngsters. Furthermore, the uses a particular teacher may understand and approve of may be uniquely unsuitable as a vehicle for teaching kids about computers. I interviewed an applicant for a teaching position at The Children's Computer School who was an expert in computer graphics. We thought his interests would mesh nicely with those of our students who were interested in game programs with graphics displays. Now you should know first that the programming of graphics varies from one machine to the next. With some operating systems the graphics programming is similar in structure to normal string and numeric manipulation programs. In other machines it is necessary to operate at the machine-language level. Even though our machines supported graphics programs written in BASIC, the teacher's skills were in machine-language programming. In two weeks we discovered the mismatch of student and teacher interest and skill. In a school in which this teacher operated without supervision, the student enrollment would drop until the principal decided that computers were not for his students.

Before I proceed with my suggestions about how to address some of the issues of computers and education, let us recall my comments from the Preface. There I said that this book was not for microcomputer experts. It is aimed toward you and your children, as well as any others, including those in the educational and teaching professions, who care to examine these issues without technical background. In order to accomplish this goal I have chosen to limit the depth of discussion but not to restrict its breadth. I hope that educators and teachers will examine the contents of this book in order to acquaint themselves with this new technology. It must be stressed, however, that the pedagogical conclusions are not the result of educational research. Rather they are the distillation of extensive experience at The Children's Computer School. My educational advice and assertions should be taken for what they are—informed opinion and reasoned hypothesis.

A computer course represents either or both of these two paths: an attempt to use computers to teach standard skills, or teaching the use of computers by teaching how to program. Both these

purposes can be advanced by the presence of computers in schools. What then are the principles that must be followed to make their use valuable? Our experience leads us to several important considerations. The first of these concerns the access to high-quality instructional programs for supporting regular subject matter instruction. As we have seen, the best opinion in this area suggests that such material is rare in the marketplace. The development of software that can teach obviously requires someone who can teach the subject matter and someone who can program the computer. Ideally, these two people should be in the same body. But how can we find teachers who can program or programmers who can teach? The answer seems clear. Until we have succeeded in producing a generation of people who are as familiar with computers as they are with books and typewriters, we will not find the master teachers who can develop this course software. We need to wait until our teachers can program before we can expect to see programs that can teach.

This point suggests that if we want to exploit our limited resources most effectively at this time in the history of microcomputers and education, we should attend to instruction in programming. This leads to a second set of questions and a second set of principles. In order to teach kids (and adults) to write computer programs, they must be sitting at a computer. This is a skill like any other and must be learned in the same way. We do not teach children arithmetic by telling them about it; we teach it by having them do it, either with paper and pencil, or more and more today, with a calculator. We do not teach spelling by distributing a dictionary and having children read it; we teach spelling by having children write.

165

Kids and Computers

All teachers have known since the beginning of history that you learn how to do things by doing them. The same truth holds for computer programming. You learn how to program by writing programs.

When I say that a child must sit at a computer in order to learn to use it, I mean that literally. I do not mean that two children, for example, can share a computer. I have never seen an effective learning session occur for the child who did not have a machine and merely watched. Indeed, at one of our early "open house" parties I had a machine broken by a fall from the worktable when the interest of one child who could not get to the keyboard became so overpowering that she tried to take the machine away from the boy who was using it. Since that time, even during demonstrations, the one-on-one rule applies. One child per computer! There is simply no other way to do it.

In order to learn how to program, the student must share the environment with a teacher. I know that a good ratio of students to teachers is one to one. I also know that this is unfeasible as a mechanism for generating growth in the number of people who know how to program. If a one to one ratio is too small, what is too large? In our school we have determined that class size alone is not critical but that the needed number of teachers in each class is at least two. This means that as soon as you get past one student per teacher, you must have at least two teachers in the same classroom. Our general principle is that classes larger than four must have two teachers present. Even with such small classes, it is usually the case that two teachers are present, except in the most advanced courses. We usually assign a master teacher at the front of the class who handles the major part of the academic instruction. A second teacher is stationed in the class in a position toward the rear of the classroom where he or she can see the screens of all the pupils. With this arrangement, confusions can be nipped in the bud. The second teacher who spots an impending error can catch it, sometimes before the error has been entered. Without the second teacher the class flounders. These principles apply with equal force to computer camps as well as schools. One cannot treat computer instruction by analogy to "nature studies." If the child expects to learn something significant, the camp must organize and implement a curriculum as coherent as that of a regular school. For just fooling around with a machine, as many older and more sophisticated kids do, these rules obviously do not apply. However, structure in the presentation of computer knowledge is just as important as it is in other disciplines.

Contrary to what may seem common sense, the size of the class cannot get larger as the students advance to higher grades. You might think that an advanced class would need less individual attention and therefore could be larger. That is not the case. The advanced classes in our school are often cut back by our dean because he thinks these kids need more, not less, attention. As far as maximum size is concerned, we have standardized on classes of less than 16. Indeed classes larger than 12 are less than optimal. If your school is very rich, and has a classroom with 30 computers in it, watch out: Some children in that class are not learning.

All these features of a sound computer-programming education are meaningless without a tried and proven curriculum. Curriculum development and the validation of the curriculum by extrinsic tests may be the largest budget item to a school for computer instruction. What you should expect from a curriculum is that it can produce students who demonstrate objectively that between 85% and 95% of them show mastery at a defined level of programming skill. At The Children's Computer School we have developed benchmark program exercises that test reliably the quality and quantity of a student's knowledge at each of the four levels of programming skill that we cover. These tests make use of various features of our computers to test in a "friendly" way. Our students often do not even recognize that what they are doing is taking a test. Without such yardsticks, the quality of the instruction is unknown. We use these tests not only to evaluate our students but also to help us in teacher assignments.

I received a complaint from one of my teachers of intermediate programming that the students in her class were not well-motivated or knowledgeable in fundamentals. Test scores confirmed the fact that her students were not up to standards. We tried two tactics. First she was reassigned to a beginning class. That class also failed to meet standards. Then she was assigned to an advanced class. The advanced class took off; she bloomed with regained self-confidence. Obviously, testing the students tests the teachers as well. By judicious analysis of student performance, teacher effectiveness can be checked, and teachers can be assigned to tasks they do best and enjoy most.

Our classes meet weekly either after school or on weekends. Our school is like a school that teaches gymnastics, music, or other extracurricular activities. It is not simply a form of late-afternoon entertainment. Consequently, in addition to the in-class curriculum, we needed, and consequently have developed, outside assignments that children and adults can do to enhance other aspects of computer literacy besides hands-on programming. These materials help to ensure that the student retains the material that is learned in class and that these materials can be extended or generalized to other kinds and styles of problems. Such "homework" assignments must be neatly dovetailed into the ongoing study plan, or they create confusions that slow down the primary task.

The father of one of our older girls took it on himself to review the homework materials that his daughter brought from school. As a highly regarded computer systems analyst he (justifiably) decided to improve our material. Unhappily, he did not inform the teacher, and when his daughter started to perform below par, it took an interview with the dean to find out what had happened. The father knew how to bypass the programming problem his daughter was trying to solve by using more advanced code. This would be much like someone telling you that your looping program was bad because you were using a loop counter and a GOTO command instead of FOR . . . NEXT. If you had never heard of FOR . . . NEXT, things could get sticky—and they did for this child. It all straightened out when the father enrolled in one of our adult courses. He could, of course, have instructed our teacher in the complexities of large mainframe computer programming. But he was a pussycat in class and now extolls the virtues of microcomputers for the executives in his company, one of the largest computer manufacturers in the world.

And finally as my last contribution to your consumer orientation about schools, a word about class length. How long should a class last? When we first started out, we thought that young children would become satiated fairly quickly if they were doing more with a computer than playing games. We started our programs with hour-long classes. What happened is obvious now, but it wasn't then. The four-to-five-o'clock class started to overlap the five-fifteen to six-fifteen class. We had allowed 15 minutes between classes for students to get their coats and hats and other materials together, but the break after class grew later and later. This was especially so in the intermediate and advanced classes. After all, if you almost have the code right, you need to give the program a test run. This always generates a syntax error, which you know if you correct will make everything okay. Once corrected, that error lets a later error show up, and before you know it the class has been over for 20 minutes. Now some strange guy is standing next to you looking over your shoulder and asking, "When are you going to finish?" Our classes now run for 2 hours, and we have not had a single complaint.

So my final view is simplicity itself: You and your child should learn to program a microcomputer. You should learn, if possible, in a school setting. The school you choose should adhere to as many as possible of the good practices I have described. Finally, you should get a microcomputer of your own and enter the future together with your child at the morning of a new age.

Glossary

ANSI	Also ASI; American National Standards Institute. Expert committees that establish commercial and government standards. An ANSI committee is currently working on a BASIC standard.
ASCII	American Standard Code for Information Interchange. A code that changes letters and symbols into numbers; for example, A = 65, Z = 90, a = 97.
BASIC	The most popular and widely used computer programming language. The BASIC commands used in this book are listed on pages 177-178.
baud	A measure of the speed of transmission of digital data. Approximately equal to bits per second, but actually the rate of change of the state of the transmission line per second.
binary digits	The numbers, 0 (zero) and 1 (one) in a system of arithmetic used by computers. The numbers can be represented as an electrical current, 1 if it is there, 0 if not.
bit	The unit of information. A bit is a 0 (zero) or a 1 (one). The name is a contraction of BInary digiT.
bootstrapping	Loading the operating system of a computer into RAM from a mass storage device—a floppy disk or cassette drive.
bubble memory	A nonvolatile (permanent) memory consisting of magnetically encoded information that is very densely packed on a chip.
bus	Control paths from the CPU to the input-output ports and to the RAM memory of the computer.
byte	A binary number 8 bits (binary digits) long. There are exactly 256 different bytes.

Kids and Computers

calculator keyboard A computer input keyboard made of keys more like those on a calculator than on a typewriter.

cathode-ray tube (CRT) An output system consisting of a TV-like tube on which the letters, numbers, or graphic output of a computer can be displayed.

central processing unit The CPU is the main component of a computer. It is the chip that performs all of the fundamental logical and numerical calculations.

chip A sliver of silicon, etched photographically into electrical circuits, that works to perform various functions in a variety of devices such as digital watches, computers, auto ignitions, etc.

circuit board A plastic board that serves to support and interconnect a collection of chips and other devices that make up a complicated electronic device such as a computer.

CMOS A memory chip that retains its information with only a very small electric current flowing through it. Such memory is often used in pocket calculators and computers so that they retain information even after they are switched "off," unlike the RAM in a microcomputer.

COBOL A programming language often used for business or commercial programs.

computer *See* digital computer.

computer language Words or symbols that the computer accepts as instructions or commands. In some high-level languages the computer language uses English words for commands and instructions. *See* high-level language.

computer literacy The ability of a person to interact easily and skillfully with a computer. The term usually refers to the ability of a person to program a computer as well as operate one.

computer program/ programming A set of instructions written in a programming language that commands the computer to perform various operations on data contained in the program or supplied by the user. Programs range from those that manage business accounts to those that make the computer into a video game.

computer terminal A keyboard (for input) and a CRT or printer (for output) that connect to a computer and serve as its input-output system. Often many terminals are attached to the same shared mainframe computer.

170

conditional branches	The logical ability of a computer to do one set of operations if one condition exists and something else if another does. For example, we all use the conditional branch *go* on green and *stop* on red when we drive a car.
CONTROL key	An extra *shift* key, often marked CTRL, found on many computer keyboards that permits the regular keys to perform other specialized operations.
core (memory)	The memory of a computer that is directly addressable by the CPU, as distinct from the memory in an external mass storage system.
CPU	*See* central processing unit.
crash	A program failure that may "lockup" the computer and require that it be reset. Sometimes this means that the computer must be turned off and then on again, thereby losing all information in RAM. That's a *hard* crash.
CRT	*See* cathode-ray tube.
cursor	A marker on the CRT of a computer that shows where the information will appear when input or output is programmed. It marks the place the computer will write to the CRT.
daisy wheel printer	A printer that uses a sectored wheel with letters at the end of the spokes to print on plain paper.
dedicated CRT	A video display system that is part of the computer and not shared for use as, say, a TV. A dedicated CRT is usually a video monitor and not a TV receiver.
descenders	The existence of dots that can print below the print line on a dot-matrix printer to allow the tails of the letters like *p, g, y,* and *q* to print below the line.
digital computer	A binary digit-based information processing system that permits a CPU to connect to an addressable memory and to get and give information through dedicated input and output systems.
disk drive (floppy)	A peripheral mass storage system that permits the storage and retrieval of data and programs stored magnetically on a small flexible plastic disk.
DOS	Abbreviation for "disk operating system," a machine-language program, often stored in ROM as firmware to permit the CPU to load and store data and programs on a floppy or hard disk mass storage system.

Kids and Computers

dot matrix	A printer that uses a column of pins to print a sequence of dots on paper in such a way that the dots form letters.
END LINE key	*See* RETURN key.
ENTER key	*See* RETURN key.
exponential notation	A representation for (very large or very small) numbers as a multiplier times ten raised to some power. For example, two million is 2×10^6, which computers print as 2E+6.
firmware	Machine-language programs stored in ROM so that they are always available to the CPU. The BASIC language in many microcomputers is stored as firmware.
floppy disk (drive)	*See* disk drive.
flowcharts	Diagrams of the logical flow of a computer program using standardized block shapes to designate operations. See the example on page 148.
FORTRAN	FORmula TRANslation. A computer programming language used extensively on large machines to solve scientific and technical problems.
game paddle	An input device consisting of a small box with a rotating knob mounted on it. Turning the knob serves as input, for example, to move graphics on the CRT. *See* joystick.
hard disk (drive)	A peripheral mass storage system using a sealed rotating magnetic disk to store data and programs. Most microcomputer hard disks use a system called Winchester technology.
high-level language	A computer language that makes use of English (or other natural language) for its codes and symbols. BASIC is the best-known example of a high-level language.
IEEE 488	A parallel interface standard for connecting microcomputer peripherals to your machine.
infinite loop	A repetitive process, often done by accident, that causes the computer to continue to perform a given segment of a program indefinitely. It can only be stopped by resetting the machine or turning it off.
input	The data on which the computer operates, usually entered from the keyboard or from a mass storage system.
input ports	Places on a microcomputer to which input systems (keyboards, game paddles, joysticks) may be connected.
integrated circuit	A chip of silicon etched with electrical paths and components that permit the circuit to perform some complex function.

interface	The electrical and logical devices that permit computers and peripherals to be interconnected. *See* IEEE 488 and RS-232C.
interpreter	A programming language system that requires the computer to translate and evaluate the program code every time the program is executed. It is a moderately slow but "user friendly" way to run a program.
joystick	An input device commonly used with computer games that consists of a box with a movable rod that can be tilted in all directions to control, e.g., CRT graphics. *See* game paddle.
keyboard	An input system consisting of a standardized layout of symbols such as letters or numbers that can be entered into a computer by finger pressure on the "keys."
light pen	An input device consisting of a small rod, much like a mechanical pencil, that is used to pick up or select information from the screen.
liquid crystal (screen)	A flat display device, usually gray in color, on which alphabetic and numeric information can be displayed.
logical functions	Programming commands such as AND, OR, and NOT that serve to limit and control program flow. For example, "do this if a AND b are both true."
LOGO	A programming language designed for use by young children that may help them to learn to program, and also teaches them various geometric concepts.
loop	A program technique that permits the program to repeat some operation or sequence of commands over and over again. *See* infinite loop.
LSI	Large-scale integrated circuits. Integrated circuits that contain thousands of electronic components on a single chip of silicon. *See* integrated circuit.
machine language	A programming language that operates at the level of binary numbers. It is the primary programming language of the computer.
mainframe	A big computer without its peripherals or other components.
mass storage system	A peripheral system that can store data and programs *off-line*. Microcomputers usually use cassette decks or floppy disks for mass storage.
mathematical functions	Programming commands such as plus (+) or minus (−) that make the computer operate on numbers, e.g., add or subtract.

173

matrix | A table consisting of rows and columns, each cell, or memory box, defined by its row/column numbers. The cells may contain numbers or words.

membrane keyboard | *See* keyboard. A keyboard without separate keys. The key locations are defined by a diagram on a continuous sheet of plastic. Pressing the plastic at the picture of a key enters that key value.

memory boxes | Our name for the one-byte memory locations used by the CPU to store information and program code.

memory size | The number of memory boxes in the computer. Usually measured in units of 1024 called 1K, for Kilo.

menu | A programming system in which the operator chooses from a list the functions and procedures of the program that are to be used.

microcomputer | A computer small enough to hug. Usually refers to a computer whose CPU has an 8-bit command bus.

minicomputer | A medium-sized computer whose CPU uses a 16-bit bus. Note that some micros now use a 16-bit CPU.

modem | MOdulator-DEModulator. A peripheral device that permits a computer to talk and listen through a telephone line.

monitor (video) | A CRT used exclusively by the computer.

monolithic | A computer that contains several components, e.g., the keyboard and video monitor, in the same chassis.

numeric variable | A name (usually a letter or two) for a memory box that holds a number.

off-line memory | Another name for a peripheral mass storage system, such as floppy disks or cassette decks.

operating system | A machine-language program that permits the computer to understand commands above the level of machine language.

output | One of the main functions of the computer. The processed data or other information that the computer displays or prints.

output port | A connection that permits information from the computer to be passed to some other device.

parallel port | An input-output port that sends and receives information in (8-bit) bunches. All of the bunch goes and comes at once.

Pascal | A high-level programming language that is structured. It requires that variables and other components of the program be stated in advance rather than introduced as needed.

peripherals — Optional attachments that connect to a microcomputer, usually mass storage, printers, and modems.

phosphors — The coating on CRTs that makes them give off light when excited by a beam of electrons—usually white (P4) or green (P39).

Pixel — PIXture ELement. The smallest addressable point on the CRT of a microcomputer. The better the picture the larger the number of pixels. Usually expressed in number of rows and columns.

printer — An output device that generates a printed record of the computer output. The printer may also be used to print a list of the program code. Printers come in two styles—dot matrix and daisy wheel.

program — The coded instructions that command the operation of a computer.

qwerty keyboard — A keyboard arranged like the keyboard on an office typewriter. The letters stand for the first six keys on the second row of the machine.

RAM — Random access memory. The main memory in most microcomputers. It is used to store programs and data.

RETURN key — The key that enters the data that has been typed in from the keyboard. On some machines it is called ENTER or END LINE.

rf modulator — A device that permits the video screen output of the computer to be displayed on a TV set.

ROM — Read-only memory. The permanent memory in a microcomputer that stores the operating systems.

RS-232C — An interface protocol or standard that permits a computer to communicate with other peripheral devices. In this mode, information is sent serially, one symbol after the other.

screen editing — The capability of many computers to permit changes and adjustments to data and program code by making the changes on the screen.

screen line — The unit of information that the computer can see with a single press of the RETURN key.

scrolling — *See* vertical scrolling.

sectors — Spaces on a floppy disk at which stored information is located.

Kids and Computers

self-documented	A program that contains information displayed on the screen that explains how to use the program.
serial port	A connection on the computer than can send and receive information bit by bit. Slow but steady and simple interface.
simulation	A program that mimics some process to get answers to questions.
soft keys	Keys on the input device that are defined by the running program.
software	Another name for computer programs.
speech synthesizer	A device that generates spoken words as output.
spooling	The ability of a printer to print out data from a mass storage system while the computer is busy doing other things at the same time.
string variable	The name given to a memory box(es) holding letters or numbers that serve only as symbols and have no numerical value.
subroutines	Pieces of program that do single specific jobs many times in the same program.
subscripted variables	Names of variables (either string or numeric) that serve to identify a whole list, or matrix, of elements.
syntax error	A spelling or grammatical mistake in a computer program.
tape drive	A mass storage system that stores program or data information on magnetic tape.
terminal	*See* computer terminal.
tracks	Spaces on a floppy disk at which information is stored. *See* sectors.
transistor	A semi-conductor electronic device that replaced the vacuum tube. Transistors are the major components of a LSI circuit.
variable	The name of a memory location in the RAM memory of a computer.
vector	A list of numbers or words.
vertical scrolling	Moving data that occupy more lines than can be shown on the screen at once so that the rest of it can be seen on the screen.
video monitor	*See* monitor.
Winchester	A kind of hard disk mass storage system.
word processing	A computer program that converts the computer into an electronic typewriter and text editor.

BASIC Commands and Functions

DIRECT COMMANDS

These commands can be used without line numbers.

LIST	This command, followed by pressing the RETURN key, prints the program currently in memory—the resident program.
RUN	Followed by pressing the RETURN key begins execution of the resident program. This command makes the program begin operating.
NEW	Clears the RAM memory of the resident program, and resets all the variables to null and zero.
PRINT	When followed by numerical operations, it prints the result like a calculator, after the RETURN key is pressed. Followed by a variable name, it prints the current contents of the memory named by the variable. Followed by symbols in double quotes, it prints the symbol string.
CONT	Causes a halted program to continue running from the point it was stopped.
GOTO	When followed by a line number and the RETURN key is pressed, starts the program executing at the line number specified.
SAVE or STORE	Usually followed by the program name inside double quotes, stores or saves the program in a mass storage peripheral. Sometimes the words are prefixed by a letter that identifies the type of mass storage, e.g., CSAVE may save to a cassette deck, whereas DSAVE may save to a floppy disk.
LOAD, CLOAD	Followed by the program name within double quotes recovers a program from a mass storage system as above.

PROGRAM COMMANDS

These commands can be used with line numbers.

PRINT
Prints symbols that follow it in double quotes to the CRT or a printer. Prints the contents of the memory boxes when followed by a variable name. Prints the result of a numerical calculation. Prints a blank line if nothing follows it.

INPUT
Prints a question mark on the screen and waits for input from the keyboard to fill the variable that must follow this command.

GOTO
Sends the program to execute at the line number that must follow this command. It is an unconditional branch in the program.

LET
Fills a variable on the left of the equals sign with the contents on the right of the equals sign.

IF . . . THEN
A conditional branch command. The program must do what is to the right of the THEN part of the command if the statement to the right of the IF part is true.

DIM
Declares how many items may be referenced by the subscripted variable that follows this command.

FOR . . . NEXT
Makes a loop using a counter variable after FOR, followed by the start and end of the count. The return of the loop is given by NEXT followed by the counter variable name.

GOSUB . . . RETURN
Makes an unconditional branch to the line number following GOSUB. Executes program at new line number until RETURN, where program returns to the line after the GOSUB command.

READ . . . DATA
READ followed by a variable name acts like an INPUT command, except that it takes its data from a program line that begins with the DATA command. Data are entered in the DATA line separated by commas.

END
Stops program execution and returns control of the computer to the keyboard.

Answers to CompuQuizzes

COMPUQUIZ #1   Chapter 2

1. input, output, CPU, memory
2. read-only memory
3. cassette tape
4. 8
5. random access memory
6. 32,000
7. false
8. typewriter keyboard
9. CRT or video or TV

COMPUQUIZ #2   Chapter 5

1. erases program from memory
2. program is displayed on screen
3. 8
4. $
5. no—string variables do not permit calculations
6. starts the program
7. END

COMPUQUIZ #3   Chapter 9

1. 19

2. LEN ( )

3. a numeric variable that gets 1 added to it each time through the loop

4. to the next line

5. (a) a list of variables with a common first name, like A$"   ". Each variable has a different last number, for example, A$(6).

5. (b) Obviously!

6. when you use subscripted variables with more than ten items

7. (a) a variable table, like B(3,5) where the 3 subscript shows the row, and the 5 subscript shows the column

7. (b) use it to make a table of numbers or words

References

Magazines

BYTE
BYTE Publications Inc., 70 Main St., Peterborough, NH 03458

COMPUTE
Small System Services, Inc., P.O. Box 5406, Greensboro, NC 27403

MICRO
Micro Ink, Inc., Chelmsford, MA 01824

Personal Computing
Hayden Publishing Co., Inc., 50 Essex St., Rochelle Park, NJ 07662

Popular Computing
BYTE Publications Inc., 70 Main St., Peterborough, NH 03458

Books

Coan, James S. *Basic BASIC: An Introduction to Computer Programming in BASIC.* Rochelle Park, NJ: Hayden Publ. Co., 1978.

Evans, Christopher. *The Mighty Micro.* London: Coronet Books, 1980.

Lien, David A. *The BASIC Handbook.* San Francisco: Compusoft, 1978.

Papert, Seymour. *Mindstorms.* New York: Basic Books, 1980.

Some Common BASIC Programs, 2nd Ed. Berkeley: Osborne & Asso., Inc., 1978.

Index

Note: Specific models of equipment and components will be found under name of manufacturer.

Programming (*cont.*)
 output formatting, 101-3
  See also Direct commands; Program
   commands; *and specific commands*
Programming codes, *see* Codes, programming
Programming languages, *see* Language(s)
Programs (software), 68-69, 82-92
 add-on ROM, 56, 60-61, 86
 CAI, 16
 chained, 92
 cost of, 64, 69, 83
 documentation and, 85, 89-92
 how to run, 86-92
 and learning computer operation, 85
 modification of, 84
 piracy of, 84-85
 "teaching," utility of, 164
 transportability of, 86
Prompt, 73-75, 79
  See also Cursor
Protocols, 119, 121
Punched cards, 12
Punched paper-tape devices, 58

Quasar HK 2500 pocket computer, 122
QUBE system, 158
Question mark (?), 73-76, 79, 108
Quotation marks, 97-98, 109
Qwerty keyboard, 26, 27

Radiation risks, 39-42, 44, 51
Radio Shack microcomputers, 13, 21, 30, 146
 Color Computer, 30, 116, 117, 124, 125
 service network for, 127
 TRS-80 model II, 52
 TRS-80 model III, 31, 39-40, 52, 116, 117, 126
 TRS-80 Model PC-2 pocket computer, 121-23
RAM (random-access memory; read-write
  memory), 25, 27, 28, 30, 55-57, 66
 amount of, as factor in choice of computer, 117
 BASIC interpreter in, 69, 120
 cassette storage and, 58
 CMOS chip, 122-23
 definition of, 24, 56-57
 NEW (or SCRATCH) command and, 71,
  74, 80, 87
Random (RND) function, 130, 131

Random-access memory, *see* RAM
READ . . . DATA command, 145
Read-only memory, *see* ROM
Read-write memory, *see* RAM
Registers of CPU, 57
REPEAT command (in LOGO), 150
RESET key, *see* BREAK key
RETURN (or ENTER or END LINE) key,
  72-75, 79, 95-96, 100, 104, 145
Reverse video display mode, 44
rf modulator, 117
RIGHT command (in LOGO), 150
RIGHT string function, 132, 133
RND function, 130, 131
Robots, industrial, 162-63
ROM (read-only memory), 28, 55-56, 66
 add-on, 56, 60-61, 86
 BASIC interpreter in, 69, 114, 120
 comparison program in, 87
 definition of, 24, 30, 55
 diagnostic programs in, 66
 extra, installation of, 86
RS-232C transmission protocol, 121
RUN command, 74, 75, 80, 87, 89, 90, 94,
  96, 100, 104, 107, 129, 130

SAVE (or STORE) command, 129
Schockley, William, 12
Schools
 approach to computers of, 164-65
 as best setting for learning to program,
  163-64
  See also Children's Computer School
SCRATCH, *see* NEW command
Screen editing, 52, 71, 114, 127
Scrolling, 52, 101, 102
Sectors (of disk), 59
Self-documentation, 89-92
Semicolon (;) as separator or delimiter, 76,
  101-2, 108
Serial transmission, 120-21
Service guarantees, 126, 127
Sex and computer skills, 20, 44
Shannon, Claude, 24, 66
Sharp PC-1500 pocket computer, 121-23
Simulation, 17-18
 paper, 104, 107
SIN (sine) function, 130

For more information on Kids & Computers:

CLUBS and FACILITIES

Send for additional free literature

**The Children's Computer School
21 West 86th Street
New York, N.Y. 10024**

Please enclose a stamped self-addressed
envelope, and be sure to include your
  Name:
  Address:
  City:
  State: Zip Code:
  Telephone No. (area code)

When you write, tell us if you already own a computer, and if so,
what make and model it is. We will use that information to send you a
free comprehensive list of software for your machine.

Computer Manufacturers

We have evaluated many of the machines offered by the manufacturers listed
below, and we will send you our evaluations on request. Be sure to indicate
your primary intended use, e.g., word processing, school work, business
projects, etc. These computer manufacturers and others mentioned in
Chapter 8 can all supply descriptive literature about their machines.

Apple Computer Inc.
10260 Bandley Drive
Cupertino, CA 95014

Atari Manufacturing Co.
1265 Borregas Ave.
Sunnyvale, CA 94086

Commodore Business Machines
681 Moore Road
King of Prussia, PA 19406

Hewlett-Packard Inc.
1000 N.E. Circle Blvd.
Corvallis, OR 97330

Radio Shack/Tandy Corp.
1300 Tandy Center
Fort Worth, TX 76102

Texas Instruments
P.O. Box 725, Dept. 59
Lubbock, TX 79491

Notes

Notes